HOW TO
HEAR YOUR
ANGELS

Other Hay House Books by Doreen Virtue

Books/Kits/Oracle Board

The Miracles of Archangel Gabriel (available May 2013)

Mermaids 101

Flower Therapy (with Robert Reeves)

Mary, Queen of Angels

Saved by an Angel

The Angel Therapy® Handbook

Angel Words (with Grant Virtue)

Archangels 101

The Healing Miracles of Archangel Raphael

The Art of Raw Living Food (with Jenny Ross)

Signs from Above (with Charles Virtue)

The Miracles of Archangel Michael

Angel Numbers 101

Solomon's Angels (a novel)

My Guardian Angel (with Amy Oscar)

Angel Blessings Candle Kit (with Grant Virtue; includes booklet, CD, journal, etc.)

Thank You, Angels! (children's book with Kristina Tracy)

Healing Words from the Angels

Realms of the Earth Angels

Fairies 101

Daily Guidance from Your Angels

Divine Magic

How to Give an Angel Card Reading Kit

Angels 101

Angel Guidance Board

Goddesses & Angels

Crystal Therapy (with Judith Lukomski)

Connecting with Your Angels Kit (includes booklet, CD, journal, etc.)

Angel Medicine

The Crystal Children

Archangels & Ascended Masters

Earth Angels

Messages from Your Angels

Angel Visions II

Eating in the Light (with Becky Prelitz, M.F.T., R.D.)

The Care and Feeding of Indigo Children

Healing with the Fairies

Angel Visions

Divine Prescriptions

Healing with the Angels

"I'd Change My Life If I Had More Time"

Divine Guidance

Chakra Clearing

Angel Therapy®

The Lightworker's Way

Constant Craving A–Z

Constant Craving

The Yo-Yo Diet SyndromeLosing Your Pounds of Pain

Audio/CD Programs

Angel Therapy® Meditations

Archangels 101 (abridged audio book)

Fairies 101 (abridged audio book)

Goddesses & Angels (abridged audio book)

Angel Medicine (available as both 1- and 2-CD sets)

Angels among Us (with Michael Toms)

Messages from Your Angels (abridged audio book)

Past-Life Regression with the Angels

Divine Prescriptions

The Romance Angels

Connecting with Your Angels

Manifesting with the Angels

Karma Releasing

Healing Your Appetite, Healing Your Life

Healing with the Angels

Divine Guidance

Chakra Clearing

DVD Program

How to Give an Angel Card Reading

Oracle Cards (divination cards and guidebook)

Talking to Heaven Mediumship Cards (with James Van Praagh; available November 2013)

Archangel Power Tarot Cards (with Radleigh Valentine; available October 2013)

Flower Therapy Oracle Cards (with Robert Reeves; available September 2013)

Indigo Angel Oracle Cards (with Grant Virtue; available July 2013)

Angel Dreams Oracle Cards (with Melissa Virtue)

Mary, Queen of Angels Oracle Cards

Angel Tarot Cards (with Radleigh Valentine and Steve A. Roberts)

The Romance Angels Oracle Cards

Life Purpose Oracle Cards

Archangel Raphael Healing Oracle Cards

Archangel Michael Oracle Cards

Angel Therapy® Oracle Cards

Magical Messages from the Fairies Oracle Cards

Ascended Masters Oracle Cards

Daily Guidance from Your Angels Oracle Cards

Saints & Angels Oracle Cards

Magical Unicorns Oracle Cards

Goddess Guidance Oracle Cards

Archangel Oracle Cards

Magical Mermaids and Dolphins Oracle Cards

Messages from Your Angels Oracle Cards

Healing with the Fairies Oracle Cards

Healing with the Angels Oracle Cards

Available at local bookstores, or may be ordered by visiting

Hay House USA:
www.hayhouse.com®

Hay House Australia:
www.hayhouse.com.au

Hay House UK:
www.hayhouse.co.uk

Hay House South Africa:
www.hayhouse.co.za

Hay House India:
www.hayhouseco.in

Doreen's website:
www.AngelTherapy.com

HOW TO HEAR YOUR ANGELS

DOREEN VIRTUE

HAY HOUSE, INC.

Carlsbad, California • New York City

London • Sydney • Johannesburg

Vancouver • Hong Kong • New Delhi

Library of Congress Control Number: 2006935087

ISBN: 978-1-4019-1705-0

15 14 13 12   15 14 13 12
1st edition, November 2007
12th edition, December 2012

Contents

Introduction: A Brief Note about This Book vii

Chapter 1: Who the Angels Are 1

Chapter 2: About Our Deceased Loved Ones 23

Chapter 3: Messages from Children in Heaven 35

Chapter 4: How to Know If It's Truly
Your Angels or Your Imagination 45

Chapter 5: How to Feel Your Angels 63

Chapter 6: How to Recognize and Receive
Divine Ideas and Profound Thoughts . . .83

Chapter 7: How to Hear Your Angels 107

Chapter 8: How to See Your Angels 123

Chapter 9: Receiving Messages from Your Angels . . 153

Afterword: Letting Heaven Help You 167

Endnotes. 171

About the Author 173

INTRODUCTION

A BRIEF NOTE ABOUT THIS BOOK

I originally wrote much of the material in this book for *Messages from Your Angels*. That work focused on channeled messages from the angelic realm, with the guidance in the following chapters almost buried in the back, but I always wanted it to be a separate book.

The information in this book is required reading for my Angel Therapy Practitioner® students as part of their certification process. It summarizes many of the processes we conduct in my classes, as well as in some of my one-day workshops.

I have a clear vision of the future of our world, and it's very positive. I see everyone listening to their angels' loving guidance and becoming more peaceful, healthy, and happy as a result. As a former psychotherapist, I've found that talking to our guardian angels is the quickest route to attaining inner peace and happiness. Their healing abilities exceed all of the human-made therapy methods I learned during my university training and clinical experiences. My prayer is that everyone takes the time to hear their angels.

Since 1995, I've taught workshops worldwide about connecting to, healing with, and listening to angels. This book is a result of the experiences I've had in teaching people of all backgrounds and ages. I've found that everyone has the ability to hear angels if they'll just trust and let go of doubts. If you'll use the methods I outline, you'll be able to do just that.

I'm with you in spirit every step of the way!

With Love and Angel Blessings,
Doreen Virtue

Chapter One

Who the Angels Are

The word *angel* means "messenger." Angels bring messages from the Divine Mind of our Creator. They're gifts to us from God, sent to help us remember our Divine nature, to be loving and kind, to discover and polish our talents for the betterment of the world, and to keep us out of harm's way before our time. They also guide us in the areas of relationships, health, career, and even finances.

Your angels are with you to enact God's plan of harmony. They help calm you, because one person at a time leads to a world of peaceful people, which equates to a world at peace. That's why your angels desire to assist you in any way that will lead you to serenity. You aren't bothering them or wasting their time if you ask for "small" favors. They know that minor irritants often add up to major stress, so it's their great pleasure to help you with anything that stands in your way.

Now while it's true that challenges do make us grow, the angels also say that peace leads to even bigger growth spurts. Through tranquility, our schedules and creativity are more open to giving service, and our bodies operate in a healthy fashion. Our relationships thrive and blossom, and we're shining examples of God's love.

Every once in a while, I'll receive a letter from someone accusing me of worshiping angels. The letter writer emphasizes that we're only supposed to venerate *God*.

I always respond in the same way: with love. We all make the mistake of assuming something about another person without checking the facts. Anyone who has read one of my books, listened to one of my audio programs, or attended one of my workshops realizes that I emphasize that all glory *does* go to God. The angels certainly don't want to be worshiped. And I absolutely never suggest that we should do so.

That being said, here's a gentle reminder: God is everywhere. The Divine is within you, within me, and definitely within all of the angels. Some of my audience members who have a hard time with organized religion don't want to hear this. Perhaps a woman's father abused her, so she rejects all father figures—even God. (Of course, God is an androgynous force Who is both our spiritual Mother and Father, although I use male pronouns to avoid awkward Him/Her constructions.) Or maybe some member of an organized religion did a man harm, so he rejects anything smacking of faith, even his spirit guides and angels. Or it could be that the Divine is just illogical to another person, so she stops thinking about anything spiritual. Perhaps someone else feels guilty because of his lifestyle, and deep down he fears that God may "punish" him, so he tries to block out all awareness of a Higher Power. Or, maybe a woman fears that God will try to control her and push her into a lifestyle devoid of fun.

Some people ask me whether it's okay to speak directly to God or to the angels, or whether this is blasphemous. I certainly prescribe that we follow our personal beliefs. However, if God, the ascended masters, and the angels are truly one, then why would it be wrong to talk directly to them? Aren't you merely accepting a gift that Heaven has bestowed upon you? You and your angels aren't conspiring against God in some sort of mutinous plot. The angels (as well as your Higher Self) will never defy God's will, so there's no chance that you might make a mistake.

The angels are aware of your "dream of fear," as well as the truth of Divine affection. God, being all-loving, has no awareness of anything *but* love. The Creator can tell when your consciousness is shut away from Him and that you're having a bad dream, but He can't tell what its content is. That would require God to be less than 100 percent love.

The angels are a bridge between the truth and the nightmarish illusion of problems. They can help bring you back from that horror into your happy waking state of health, happiness, peace, and abundance. They work in conjunction with your Higher Self and the soul you're spiritually aligned with, such as Jesus, Moses, Quan Yin, the Holy Spirit, Buddha, Yogananda, or whomever. The angels don't judge your beliefs. Rather, they work within your present thoughts as a way to reach you.

A Course in Miracles says that God doesn't help us out during times of trouble because He sees no need (seeing only love and perfection, not the illusion of lack or problems). However, God *does* send helpers when we think we're in trouble. It's not that we're ignored; it's just that the Divine way of assisting us is to know that everything is already resolved in truth.

But just in case we insist on staying asleep to that fact, God created angels to help us find our way out of the nightmares we create.

The angels have told me that we wouldn't need them if we stayed fully aware of love's presence at all times. Since we "channel surf" between varying degrees of fear and love, however, God sends us Heavenly assistants to help us out.

When It's a Person's Time to Go

In my work as a clairvoyant medium who converses with the deceased, and as a researcher who has reviewed hundreds of cases of near-death experiences, I'm convinced that we can't die unless it's our time to go. We can mess up our lives or our bodies, and we can have close calls, but unless it's right for us, death can't ring our doorbell.

Each of us creates a basic life plan prior to incarnation. This includes the form our life purpose will take (such as being a writer, healer, musician, teacher, and so on). It also outlines some of the major experiences and relationships we'll encounter.

This isn't a fatalistic philosophy. We each choose these experiences prior to coming to Earth—our free will is entirely involved. Plus, we don't plan our whole lives ahead of time—that would be boring! Instead, we only devise the major intersections and some overall themes, such as the personal lessons we'll learn during our incarnation (patience or compassion, for example).

We also come up with two, three, or more ages when we'll exit the physical plane and return to our Divine Home—for instance, the ages of 18, 47, and 89. Each time one of these years comes up for you, you'll have an intersection occur (such as a near-accident, disease, or suicidal thought) that will give you the option of going to Heaven or staying here. Most people opt for longer lives so that they can be with their earthly families for a generation or two. But some plan early exits, and they return Home before their bodies reach full maturity. Even though they were physically small, their souls may have been older than yours or mine when they left the Earth plane.

Your inner wisdom knows the different times when you contracted to depart—and you can discover what they are by simply asking your Higher Self, "What age will I be when I leave this physical body?" Most of you will automatically hear (with your inner ears) three ages. Some of you will see

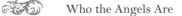

numbers in front of you, while still others will receive nothing—usually because you subconsciously don't want to know the answer.

There are those who will hear an age that is just around the corner and then get nothing else. This can mean that your time is almost up, or that your ego is running rampant, trying to scare you. After all, it operates from fear. Ninety-nine percent of the time, you have older ages coming up, but your fear is preventing you from hearing those numbers. Relaxation, breathing exercises, and meditation can help you receive the answers accurately.

The committee that helps us draw up this plan includes the beings who will stay by our side as our guardian angels and spirit guides. We each have at least two guardian angels from start to finish; everyone also has at least one spirit guide, and usually more. Guardian angels are those beings who haven't incarnated as humans (unless they were *incarnated* angels, a topic beyond the scope of this work, but which is covered in my books *Realms of the Earth Angels* and *Earth Angels*). Your spirit guides are usually your deceased loved ones. When you're young, they consist of relatives who passed away before you were born.

These beings help keep us on track in fulfilling our purpose and learning our personal lessons. They also help us avoid messing up our lives or bodies. They intervene, without needing our permission, if we're about to be killed before it's our time to die. If one of our "intersection" ages comes up, where we could opt out, the angels and guides assist us with our decision making. Usually, if we haven't yet fulfilled our purpose and learned our lessons, and especially if we have living loved ones, we'll choose to stick around until our next intersection age comes up.

I learned firsthand that the angels can only help us to the degree to which we'll allow them. In 1995, a loud and clear male angel's voice warned me that unless I put the top up on my convertible car, it would be stolen. For a number of reasons, I didn't follow this guidance, and I ended up in an armed carjacking one hour later. Then the angel told me to scream with all my might. This time I listened, and my cries attracted the attention of people who came to my rescue.

Both times when the angel attempted to help me, I had the choice to listen or to ignore him. If I'd ignored his second warning—"Scream with all your might"— I don't know if I'd still be alive today. But I do know this: If I'd perished, at least I would have known that the angels did their best to intervene and prevent my death. I've seen this same type of free choice in everyone I've spoken to—both those who have had a brush with death, and those who have succumbed and then spoken to me from the Other Side.

Guardian Angels

As I mentioned, guardian angels are personally assigned to you for your entire life. Again, they've never lived as humans on Earth unless they were "incarnated angels" (ones who take human form, either briefly or for a lifetime).

Regardless of faith, character, or lifestyle, everyone has at least two guardian angels—whether someone listens to them, though, is an entirely different matter. One is your extroverted "nudging" angel, who pushes you to make choices in keeping with your highest self. She knows your talents and potential and encourages you to shine brightly in all ways. (I'll address angels' genders in a little bit.)

The other guardian angel is much quieter in her voice and energy level. She comforts you when you're sad, lonely, or disappointed. She hugs you when you don't get the job or home that you desperately wanted, and calms you when your Friday-night date doesn't show up.

You can have more than two guardian angels—in fact, most people I meet have many around them. However, my sampling comes from individuals who attend my workshops; and generally, those who appreciate angels attract *more* of them. It's not that angels are biased in favor of their fans; it's just that those who are angelically inclined tend to ask for additional help. This request is always fulfilled, no matter who makes it.

Our angels *do* have gender energies that make them look and act distinctively male or female. However, each of us has Divine companions with different ratios of male to female. So you might have three males and one female, while your sister has two females.

All angels really do have wings and a Heavenly appearance, similar to the look of Renaissance paintings reproduced on holiday cards and in religious art. They don't use these wings for transportation in my experience, as I've never seen an angel flapping. I've seen them enfold a person in their wings for comfort, and that's the only purpose that they have, from what I've witnessed.

One time, the angels told me that the only reason they have wings is due to our Western expectations. They said, *The original painters of angels mistook our aura of light for wings, so they depicted us with wings in their paintings, and we appear to you this way so that you will know that it is us, your angels.*

Interestingly, the guardian angels surrounding people of Eastern religious orientations, such as those who practice Buddhism or Hinduism, usually don't have wings. Their angels are akin to *bodhisattvas* (enlightened ascended beings), performing the same role as the Western guardian angels: to love, protect, and guide the person to whom they're assigned. The only exceptions are those Easterners who come from eclectic or New Age backgrounds. These individuals have large groups of spiritual helpers around them. Typically, such a person will tell me, "I called upon *everyone* in Heaven to surround and help me!"

The Archangels

The archangels oversee the guardian angels. They're usually larger, stronger, and more powerful. Depending upon your belief system, there are four, seven, or an infinite number of archangels. We will meet additional archangels in the near future, almost like discovering new planets or solar systems.

The archangels are nondenominational, and they help anyone, regardless of their religious or nonreligious background. They're able to be with each one of us, individually and simultaneously, because they're beyond space and time restrictions. Imagine what your life would be like if you could be in many different places at the same time! Well, the angels say that the only reason we don't experience bilocality is because we *believe* that we can only be in one location at a time. Soon, we'll learn how to lift that restriction, according to them.

The reason why I emphasize this point is that some people worry that if they call upon Archangel Michael, for example, they might be pulling him away from a more "important" assignment. This is how we project our human limitations! The fact is that the archangels and the ascended masters can be with anyone who desires their assistance and have a completely unique experience with each being. So know that you can call upon the archangels by mentally asking them to help you. No formal prayers are necessary.

The exact number of archangels who exist depends upon which belief system or spiritual text you consult. The Bible, Koran, Testament of Levi, Kabbalah, Third Book of Enoch, and writings of Dionysius all list and describe differing numbers and names.

Suffice it to say that there are many archangels, although I usually only highlight Michael, Raphael,

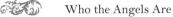

Uriel, and Gabriel in my books and workshops. However, the others have lately been urging me to involve them in my life and work, so here are some additional descriptions of archangels and how you may wish to work with them. The different gender designations come from my interactions with these archangels. Since angels and archangels don't have physical bodies, their gender relates to the energy of their specialties. For example, Archangel Michael's strong protectiveness is very male, while Jophiel's focus upon beauty is very female.

- **Archangel Ariel**'s name means "lion or lioness of God." Ariel is known as the Archangel of the Earth because she works tirelessly on behalf of the planets. She oversees the elemental kingdom, and helps in the healing of animals, especially the nondomesticated kind. Call upon Ariel to become better acquainted with the fairies, to help with environmental concerns, or to heal an injured wild bird or other animal.

- **Archangel Azrael**'s name means "whom God helps." Azrael is sometimes called the Angel of Death because he meets people at the time of their physical passing and escorts them to the Other Side. He helps newly crossed-over souls to feel comfortable and very loved. This archangel assists ministers of all religions and also spiritual teachers. Call upon Azrael for your deceased or dying loved ones, and also for help with your formal or informal ministry.

- **Archangel Chamuel**'s name means "he who sees God." He helps us locate important parts of our lives. Call upon Chamuel to find a new love relationship, new friends, a new job, or any lost item. Once your new situation is found, he'll help you to maintain and build it. So ask him if you need help in repairing any misunderstandings in personal or work relationships.

- **Archangel Gabriel**'s name means "God is my strength." In early Renaissance paintings, Gabriel is portrayed as a female archangel, although later writings refer to this being in masculine pronouns (perhaps because of the Council of Nicea's massive editing of scriptures). She's the messenger angel who helps all earthly messengers such as writers, teachers, and journalists. Call upon Gabriel to overcome fear or procrastination in any endeavor involving communication or any aspect of child conception, adoption, pregnancy, and early childhood.

- **Archangel Haniel**'s name means "grace of God." Call upon this angel whenever you wish to add grace and its effects (peace, serenity, enjoyment of good friends' company, beauty, harmony, and so on) to your life. You can also request aid before any event in which you desire to be the embodiment of grace, such as giving an important presentation, being interviewed for a job, or going on a first date.

- **Archangel Jeremiel**'s name means "mercy of God." He's an inspirer who motivates us to devote ourselves to spiritual acts of service. He's also involved with the process of attaining Divine wisdom. Call upon Jeremiel if you feel "stuck" spiritually and to regain enthusiasm about your spiritual path and Divine mission. Jeremiel provides comfort for emotional healing, and is wonderfully helpful with forgiveness issues.

- **Archangel Jophiel**'s name means "beauty of God." She's the patron archangel of artists who helps us see and maintain beauty in life. Call upon her before beginning any artistic project. Since Jophiel is involved in beautifying the planet by cleansing it of pollution, you can also ask her for assignments to help in this vital mission. I also call Jophiel the "Feng Shui" angel, because she can help you clear out clutter from your office, home, or even your life in general.

- **Archangel Metatron**'s name means "angel of the Presence." He's thought to be the youngest and the tallest of the archangels, and one of the two archangels who once walked upon the earth as a man (as the prophet Enoch). Metatron works with Mother Mary to help children, both living and crossed over. Call upon him for any kind of assistance you may need with your children. His intervention often involves helping youngsters open their spiritual awareness and understanding. He also helps Crystal and Indigo children keep their spiritual gifts awakened and to cope with school, home, and other aspects of life.

- **Archangel Michael**'s name means "he who is as God" or "he who looks like God." He's the archangel who releases the effects of fear from the planet and its inhabitants. He's the patron of police officers and gives all of us the courage and backbone to follow our truth and fulfill our Divine mission. Call upon Michael if you feel afraid or confused about your personal safety, your Heavenly purpose, or making a necessary life change. You can also ask him to help you fix any mechanical or electrical problems. In addition, Michael can assist you in remembering your life purpose, and then give you the courage to follow through on it.

- **Archangel Raguel**'s name means "friend of God." He's often called the Archangel of Justice and Fairness and is the champion of underdogs. Ask him for aid whenever you feel that you're being overpowered or manipulated. Raguel will intervene by giving you guidance about how to attain balanced power and fairness within the structure of your personal and community relationships. Also call upon Raguel on behalf of another person who's being treated unfairly. Raguel will also help you harmonize all of your relationships.

- **Archangel Raphael**'s name means "God heals," and he's in charge of physical healings. He helps all those dedicated to health and well-being; this extends to those who are not yet active in this field. Call upon Raphael for any injuries or illnesses related to yourself or another (including animals). Ask him to help with your healing work, including education and building a private practice. In addition, Archangel Raphael aids those who are traveling, so request that he ensures a harmonious and safe journey.

- **Archangel Raziel**'s name means "secret of God." He's said to stand very near to God, so he hears all Divine conversations about universal secrets and mysteries. He wrote these secrets into a document that he gave to Adam, which eventually ended up in the hands of the prophets Enoch and Samuel. Call upon Raziel whenever you wish to understand esoteric material (including your dreams) or to engage in alchemy or manifestation.

- **Archangel Sandalphon**'s name means "brother," because, like Archangel Metatron, he was once a human prophet (Elijah) who ascended into archangeldom. Sandolphon is the archangel of music and prayer. He assists Archangel Michael to clear away fear and the effects of fear (with music). Put on some soothing music and call upon him to dispel any spiritual confusion.

- **Archangel Uriel**'s name means "God is light." This Heavenly being pours light upon a troubling situation, which illuminates our problem-solving abilities. Call upon Uriel whenever you get into a sticky situation and you need to think clearly and find answers. Uriel also helps students and those who need intellectual assistance.

- **Archangel Zadkiel**'s name means "righteousness of God." He has long been regarded as the angel of good memory, and like Uriel, he's a great helper to students. Call upon Zadkiel to help you remember *anything,* including your own Divinity.

Ascended Masters

Ascended masters are beings who walked upon the earth as great leaders, teachers, and healers, and who continue to help us from their vantage point in the spirit world. They include the famous, such as Jesus, Moses, Buddha, Quan Yin, Mary, Yogananda, and the saints; and the not-so-famous, such as yogis who transcended physical restrictions during their lifetime, pioneering inventors, and unsung heroes. With bigger-than-life love in their hearts and a steadfast devotion to us, they help anyone who calls upon them. In my book *Archangels & Ascended Masters,* I describe these different beings in detail and discuss how to work with each one.

The Nature Angels

Often referred to as fairies, elementals, or devas, these beings are as much God's angels as are the guardian and archangels. Viewed with suspicion, though, they're often disregarded and misunderstood. I recently visited a large bookstore and happily noted all of the angel books on a shelf that was specially marked "Angels." But I wondered, *Where are the books about fairies?* I looked all around the New Age and Spirituality areas without finding one. I finally discovered them in a large section called "Mythology." I felt sad on behalf of the fairies, and I understood why I'd been given the assignment to help bring their word forward in my books and workshops.

Fairies are believed to be mischievous at best and evil at worst. Unlike guardian angels or archangels, these beings do have egos. They're denser angels who live closer to Earth, and those who live here usually do have this personality feature, after all.

The nature angels, including the fairies, are God's environmental helpers. They oversee the earth's atmosphere, landscape, bodies of water, and animals. If you're someone who respects the environment by, for instance, recycling and picking up litter, the fairies will accord you great respect. If, on top of that, you go the extra mile, such as being kind to animals and using nontoxic cleaning compounds, these spirits will be thrilled to meet and work with you.

The nature angels scan each person with whom they come into contact, and they instantly know your level of commitment to the environment. As soon as you begin communicating with them, they'll attempt to enlist you as an aide in their campaign to save our world.

Those whose life purpose involves helping animals or the environment often have fairies or other elementals near them, acting as guardian angels. These spirits are with the humans, in addition to their guardian angels and guides. I've found that they behave themselves quite well and don't interfere with their humans' free will or happiness. Their interventions are usually limited to proddings to get involved in environmental causes and to engage in free-spirited body movement. You can also read more about the elementals in my book *Fairies 101.*

Chapter Two

About Our Deceased Loved Ones

I f you've lost people whom you were close to, chances are they've spent time with you after they've crossed over, and they may even be with you on a regular basis. After all, in addition to angels, archangels, and ascended masters, you also have deceased loved ones with you to help. They may be relatives who passed before your birth, people with whom you shared a close bond, or those from your past who can teach you a special skill for your life's purpose.

When people leave this plane, they're eventually given the option of performing service work, both to expand their own spiritual progress and to help others. Some volunteer to become guides to their living loved ones. They usually elect to stay until the end of their charge's physical life. Time measurement is different in Heaven, so if you live to be 90, it feels like a much shorter time period to those on the Other Side.

These beings are with you because they care about you. In addition, you may have a similar mission with respect to the deceased loved ones who are by your side—that is, being with you is a way to vicariously fulfill their life purpose if they didn't do so while in their earthly bodies. If you were named after your dear departed Aunt Annette, chances are she's your spirit guide. Namesakes nearly always stay with you. Perhaps you were given that name because your parents intuitively realized your soul-path similarities.

So, when Aunt Annette decides to be your spirit guide, she first must go through the equivalent of a spiritual-counselor training program. In that Heavenly school, she learns how to be with you in a supportive way without interfering with your free will, how to travel the astral plane, and still be within earshot should you ever call for her help. She finds out how to communicate with you through your strongest spiritual-communication channel, such as your dreams, inner voice, gut feelings, or intellectual insights. It takes time to train to become a spirit guide. That's why recently deceased loved ones aren't with you continuously. Only someone who has gone through extensive training can be by your side night and day.

Let's say that Aunt Annette was a very successful newspaper reporter and you're an aspiring author. In fact, writing is part of your life's purpose. So when you ask Heaven, "What's my mission in life?" your aunt telepathically encourages you to write. Of course, she's only doing this because she knows what God's Divine mission is for you.

Sometimes people will ask me if it's okay to talk with the dead. They may quote from the Torah, which cautions against speaking to the dead and mediums. I can understand these warnings, because it's a mistake to turn our lives over to those who have passed on, just as it's not right to give control to those who are living.

Our Higher Self, in conjunction with our Creator, is who we want to be in charge. Our deceased loved ones can definitely help us, but they're not automatically saints, angels, or psychics just because their souls have crossed over. However, they can work in conjunction with God, the Holy Spirit, the ascended masters, and the angels to help us fulfill Divine will (which is one with our Higher Self's intentions). I think the main reason to contact these guides is for that extra boost of help they can provide, as well as to maintain or deepen our relationships with them.

I'm also asked whether we're bothering departed loved ones when we call upon them for help. Just as living people have the option to say no when they don't want to be bothered, so do those in Heaven. My experience, though, is that the departed love to be helpful. After all, they have all the time in the other-world now! And mostly, they want to help because they love you.

For Those Who Are Adopted

I'm often asked about the spirit guides of adopt-ees. I've found that these individuals have more angels and deceased loved ones with them than oth-ers do. An adopted person always has a spirit guide who's a relative from their birth family—I've never seen an exception to this. It could be a parent, sib-ling, grandparent, aunt, or uncle who's passed away. It doesn't matter whether the adopted person ever met this family member or not. The bond is there, regardless of whether a relationship was forged while both parties were living.

In addition, these folks have guides from the friends and adopted family members whom they've been with along the way. I believe that they have more angels than those who weren't adopted—for protection and to help them adjust to the life changes that result from the process of adoption.

Deepening Your Relationship with Deceased Loved Ones

"Are my departed loved ones okay?" is a question I hear continually. The reason people ask is simple: the fear that someone is in some sort of "hellish" place, literally or figuratively. Yet my readings find that 90 percent of deceased people are doing just fine, thank you. Their only discomfort has to do with you and me, especially if we're grief-stricken to the point of obsession or emotional paralysis. They're going on with their lives, and they want you to do the same. If you hold back your spiritual progress or happiness due to grief, those who have passed on are held back in similar ways.

In fact, it's safe to say that the only problem most people in Heaven have is . . . *us!* If we'd go on to live happy, productive lives, our deceased loved ones would sing and party in joyful celebration.

On the Other Side, spirits feel wonderful physically. All illness, injury, and disability disappear once

27

the body is gone. The soul is intact and in perfect health. Everyone still feels like him- or herself, but without the heaviness and pain of having earthly limitations.

In Heaven, souls feel wonderful emotionally, too. Gone are all of the financial and time constraints, and there are no more pressures or concerns (unless we're inordinately desolate and pull our departed loved ones down emotionally). Someone in Heaven is free to manifest any situation or condition, such as world travel, a beautiful home, volunteer work, and time with family and friends (living and deceased).

"But what if my departed loved ones are mad at me?" I'm frequently asked. People worry that crossed-over friends and family members are angry with them because they:

- Weren't there for the dying person toward the end of their life, or at their last dying breath

- Were involved in decisions to stop artificial life-support systems

- Are involved in lifestyle choices that they believe their deceased loved ones wouldn't approve of

- Fought with family members over inheritance issues

- Worry that they could have prevented the death or were somehow to blame

- Haven't yet found, or brought to justice, the person who's seemingly responsible for a murder or accident

- Had an argument with the person shortly before their death

The fact is, though, that during all of my thousands of readings, I've never met a deceased person who was angry about any of the above matters. In Heaven, you release a lot of the concerns that weigh you down on Earth. You have better clarity about people's true motivations, so your crossed-over loved ones have a deeper understanding of why you acted (or still do act) in certain ways. Instead of judging you, they view you with compassion. They only interfere with your behaviors (such as addictions) if they see that your lifestyle is killing you or preventing you from fulfilling your life's purpose.

And don't worry that Grandpa is watching when you shower or make love. These souls aren't voyeurs. In fact, there's some evidence that spirit guides don't see our physical selves on Earth; they perceive our energy and light bodies instead. So they simply understand your true thoughts and feelings during each circumstance.

Since spirit guides are aware of how you actually feel and think, there's no need to hide your worries from them. Let's say that you have conflicted feelings over your father's death. You're angry because Dad's incessant smoking and drinking contributed to his too-early demise. But you feel guilty, because you believe it's "wrong" to be angry at a dead person, especially your father.

Your dad knows just how you feel, because he's able to read your mind and heart from his vantage point in Heaven. Your deceased loved ones ask you to come clean with them—to have a heart-to-heart discussion about your unfinished anger, fear, guilt, and worry. You can have this conversation by writing a letter to the person who's passed away, by thinking the thoughts you want to convey, or by speaking aloud.

You can communicate with your deceased loved ones anytime and anywhere. Their souls aren't located at the cemetery; they're free to travel throughout the universe. And don't worry that you're disturbing their peace. Everyone wants to heal unfinished business in relationships, whether they're living or not, so your departed ones are just as happy and motivated about this discussion as you are.

Animal Angels

Would it surprise you to discover that among the deceased loved ones who watch over you are some of your beloved pets? Your dogs, cats, horses, and any other animals you deeply loved stay with you after their physical passing. The bond that you shared when they were living acts like a leash that keeps them eternally by your side, long after death.

When I give workshops, I tell audience members about the dogs and cats I see running and playing throughout the room. Usually we can figure out pretty quickly which dog belongs to which person, because these creatures stay by their owners' sides. These reunions, in which audience members discover that Rover is still around, are quite touching and emotional. People discover that their pets have the same personalities, appearance, and behaviors that they did while living. If the animal was playful, hyperactive, friendly, well groomed, or amazingly calm, she or he maintains these characteristics after physical death. Playful pups jump in piles of etheric leaves and chase after balls. Whether these leaves, balls, and other playthings are conjured by the dogs' imagination, I don't know.

Cats stay with their owners, too, although they usually don't stick as closely to a human's side as a dog does, due to their independence. So at my workshops, it's difficult for me to tell which felines belong to which people. I have to rely on describing the various cats running around the room, and having their owners "claim" them.

Many of my audience members report that they've seen or felt apparitions of their deceased pets. For instance, you might feel Fluffy the cat jump on your bed, or sense Red the dog lying on the couch. With your peripheral vision, you might even see your pet dart across the room. This is because the corner of your eye is more sensitive to light and movement than the front of your eye, so you often see psychic visions out of this area. When you turn to view the image from the front, though, it seems to disappear.

I've seen a few horses and even one guinea pig hanging around like guardian angels. These were beloved pets to their owners, and they continue to stand loyally next to "their people." The animals help by infusing us with their Divine energy of love, and also providing companionship that maybe only our unconscious is aware of.

I've also noticed spirit totem animals. These are eagles, wolves, and bears who circle their human's head, giving them protection and natural wisdom.

I've observed dolphins with people who are involved in oceanographic concerns, as well as unicorns around those who are highly attuned to nature and the elemental kingdom. I've never seen a pet goldfish hanging around, but then again, goldfish go through a very different sort of tube of light at the end of their lives, don't they?!

You can maintain communication with all of your deceased loved ones, including your pets, through the processes described herein.

Chapter Three

Messages from Children in Heaven

There's probably nothing more tragic than saying good-bye to a child, yet children's souls are very lively in Heaven, and they definitely live on in very happy and meaningful ways. For several years, I limited my private angel-therapy practice to giving free-of-charge readings to parents whose children had crossed over. I learned a great deal talking to these young people on the Other Side.

Losing a child brings up more guilt than just about anything I've ever witnessed. Most parents are distraught, wondering whether they could have prevented—or whether they in some way caused—their child's death. They hound themselves with "If only's": "If only I hadn't let Amy drive the car that night," "If only I'd paid more attention to Dan when he said that he was unhappy," or "If only I'd been stricter about letting Jacob stay out so late."

Of course, berating yourself won't bring your child back to life. However, I'd like to share some information with you that may help your heart heal.

— Young children have a different perspective on death. Children who are five years old or younger don't have a concept of death the way that we do. That's why it's so difficult to explain the permanence of a loved one's passing to a toddler. "But *when* is Grandpa coming back?" the child will continually ask, no matter how many times you explain that his grandfather is now in Heaven.

So, when infants and children pass over, they don't realize that they're dead. After all, they feel happy and alive. *Why is everyone crying?* they wonder. Since they don't know that they've passed on, they rush to the aid of their bereaved family members, offering etheric gifts to cheer them up. One time when I was giving a reading to a mother who had lost her four-year-old daughter, the woman began sobbing inconsolably. From the spirit world, the little girl began drawing rainbows to comfort her mom. As she handed each picture to her mother, I reported the occurrence.

"She loved painting rainbows when she was living," the mother said to me wistfully. "She knew that they always brought a smile to my face, too."

— **Children don't hold grudges in Heaven.** I've never met a deceased child (or adult, for that matter) who blames another person for their death. Even murder victims are very forgiving of their murderers, realizing that holding on to anger only hurts *them.* The person who was killed may help to incarcerate the criminal, though—not out of revenge, but to prevent additional murders from occurring.

Children who are aborted don't blame their parents, and they don't realize that they're dead, either. In fact, the souls of children who don't grow to full-term births because of abortion, miscarriage, or stillbirth stay by their mothers' sides. Those souls then have "first dibs" on the next body that the mother conceives. So, if you've lost an infant or fetus and have since had another child, chances are good that this is the same soul. If the woman doesn't conceive additional children, that soul then grows up next to the mother and acts as a spirit guide. Or, the child's spirit may enter the physical world and come into its mother's family in another way, such as adoption, or by becoming her niece or nephew.

— **A child's soul can hold great wisdom.** Even though children's bodies are small, it doesn't mean that their spirits are young, hapless, or naïve. So we need to consider that the child's soul may have had some responsibility in the timing of the death. The text of the spiritual tome *A Course in Miracles* says: "No one dies without his own consent," and I have found this to be true. Ask any nurse or doctor, and they'll tell you stories of people who died from minor illnesses because they willed themselves to. They'll also recount uplifting tales about those who decided to live, despite all medical odds going against them.

As difficult as it might be to accept, your child may have made the decision to go Home to Heaven before you were ready for him or her to leave. In my book *Angel Therapy,* I recounted that the angels said they don't understand where we got the idea that everyone is supposed to live to be 90 years old!

As I mentioned earlier, before our conception, we decide along with our angels and guides what age we will be when we pass from our physical bodies. One deceased teenage boy told me that following his car accident, he was given a life-or-death choice by his angels, who showed him the consequences of each decision. During my reading with this boy and his living mother, he said to her through me:

I gave you a gift by choosing to die, even though you may not understand it. I was shown that, if I had chosen to live, I would have been severely disabled. I realized how stressful that would have been to you, to your finances, and to me. I discovered that the stress would affect your marriage. I would have felt helpless and guilty had I chosen to live! So please forgive me, but I made the choice to leave my body. The angels showed me that, as painful as it would be for you, you would eventually recover and go on. They showed me that you and Dad would stay married and supportive of each other.

So please accept my gift. Please understand my choice! You were always proud of me in the past, and I need you to be proud of me now for this decision that I've made. Please believe me that I'm very, very happy here.

The mother told me that when her son was in the operating room following his car accident, the doctor reported that his vital signs were sporadic. "He said it was like having a tug-of-war with my son's life, where my son would come back into his body for a while, only to leave a moment later and then come back."

This woman vowed to accept her child's decision with as much grace as she could muster. I counseled her to work with prayer and a grief-support group to buoy up her faith that his death was not in vain, and to know that he was happy and at peace in Heaven.

— **All suffering is now over.** Many parents drive themselves crazy imagining that their child suffered terribly prior to their death. I won't sugar-coat it—many people do undergo physical pain and sheer terror during the process of dying. Fortunately, God's mercy has created some safeguards that help us shut down awareness of overwhelming pain. The human body will faint, the person will dissociate (go somewhere else in consciousness), or the spirit will be removed from the body before the anguish gets too horrible. I find that most parents' imaginings are ten times worse than the actual suffering the child undergoes.

— **Children are never alone in Heaven.** Grand-parents, aunts, uncles, beloved pets, and other children surround any child who has passed away. Usually, children live on the Other Side with relatives whom they knew on Earth, and/or relatives who were their spirit guides. In Heaven, you can manifest any type of home that you like, so the children there have relatively normal lives, are in comfortable homes, and are surrounded by loving family members and friends. I have never met a deceased child who was alone.

— **The vast majority of young people who commit suicide adjust very well in Heaven.** The myth is that people who commit suicide go to hell and suffer for their "sin." The movie *What Dreams May Come* with Robin Williams seemed to underscore this myth. (Although I believe the scriptwriter was making a metaphor about suicide, many people I talk to take the portrayal literally.)

Suicide *is* frowned upon in Heaven, because it's wasting a body that could be used in service of the Light. However, no one judges suicide victims, and they certainly aren't cast into any hell or dungeon. They can create their own hell-like situation through the extreme guilt they feel once they realize how much pain they caused their surviving family members. Yet the majority of deceased people I've talked to following their suicides rapidly forgive themselves and whomever they were angry with.

Angels and guides surround these individuals like mental-health counselors. Your prayers also help their spiritual upliftment and healing. Very often, they're assigned some form of community-service work such as becoming temporary spirit guides to counsel suicidal people against taking their lives.

Parental guilt seems to go hand in hand with rearing children, and this terrible feeling is certainly compounded when our children become ill, get injured, or pass away. However, *A Course in Miracles* reminds us that guilt isn't a form of love; it is actually attack in disguise. When we feel it, we're attacking ourselves and debasing the other person's free will. Guilt is often arrogance at its worst, such as when we fantasize that we could have swooped in and saved the day. Perhaps we could have, perhaps not. But what purpose does it serve to second-guess it after the fact? Our deceased loved ones, especially our children, want us to be happy. And the best route to joy that I know of is through giving service using our natural talents, passions, or interests.

This work can be a living memorial to a deceased child, something to make meaning out of the seemingly senseless death. For instance, you could plant a tree in the child's honor, organize a 5K walk to raise funds for other children in similar situations, give a speech to parents' groups on a topic relevant to your child's life and death, put an organ-donor notation on the back of your driver's license (making sure that you also inform your family about your desire to become a donor), write an article about your child, name a star after him or her, or start a fund in your child's name. Whether the effort is seemingly small or monumentally heroic, your child will appreciate it very much. He or she will likely help you with the project as well.

Life Goes On

In the next few chapters, you'll read about some methods to keep your relationship with your loved ones alive through spiritual communication. As we've seen in the last two chapters, their souls want us to continue our lives in healthy, happy, and meaningful ways. And that, perhaps, is the best living monument we could make to them.

Chapter Four

How to Know If It's Truly Your Angels or Your Imagination

little girl stares at the space near her left shoulder, having a seemingly one-sided conversation.

"Who are you talking to, sweetheart?" her mother asks.

"My angel," the girl replies matter-of-factly.

The girl's mother recounted to me later, "The funny thing is, we aren't a religious family, and we've never discussed angels in front of her. As far as I know, she hasn't had any exposure to the idea."

I've heard similar stories from parents around the world. Children are definitely more receptive to seeing and hearing their angels than the average adult. And why is that? In my research, I've found that the primary reason is that *children don't care whether the angel and its message consitute reality or fantasy.* They simply enjoy the experience without questioning its validity. Perhaps that's why a study by Dr. William MacDonald of The Ohio State University found that children had more verifiable psychic experiences than any other age-group.

We adults get so uptight about whether we're imagining an angel's presence that we often dismiss legitimate Divine guidance! If we could be as a child and suspend disbelief for a while, we could enjoy deeper and richer experiences of God and the angelic kingdom.

However, our grown-up left brain often rules the roost and demands proof and evidence. And perhaps painful experiences have made us guarded in this respect. We want guarantees that our lives really will improve before we're willing to quit our jobs and become self-employed, or leave the town where we grew up.

Fortunately, some distinguishing characteristics help us to tell true angelic experiences from wishful thinking (or fear-based energy). They occur to us through our four Divine senses: vision, hearing, thoughts, and feelings. We all receive angelic messages through these senses. However, we have one primary sense that we're particularly attuned to. For instance,

I'm a highly visual person, so most of my angelic experiences come as visions. Others might be more attuned to their gut feelings, thoughts, or inner ears.

Feeling Heaven's Messages

An emotional or physical "feeling" is the way in which most people experience their angels. When you're unsure whether you're really experiencing an angelic visit or message, check for these signs:

A True Angelic Experience Involving Feelings

Such an encounter may:

- Feel warm and cuddly, like a loving hug

- Make you feel safe, even if it's warning you of danger

- Often be accompanied by disembodied fragrances of flowers or your deceased loved one's distinct scent

- Leave an indent in the couch or bed, as if someone has just sat next to you

- Cause air-pressure or temperature changes

- Feel like someone is touching your head, hair, or shoulder

- Cause you to be sleepy or hyper afterward

- Give you a deep belief that "this is real"

- Create repetitious and consistent gut feelings to make a certain life change, or to take a certain step

- Seem as though a familiar person is next to you, such as sensing a particular deceased loved one

- Feel natural, as if the experience is coming to you freely

Imagination or False Guidance Involving Feelings

Such an experience may:

- Feel cold and prickly

- Make you afraid and panicky

- Have no sense of smell associated with it, or an unfamiliar and unpleasant smell

- Feel like someone is sexually fondling you (if this happens, immediately call upon Archangel Michael to clear the energy)

- Cause the room to feel ice-cold

- Give you a sense of being all alone

- Cause normal feelings to return quickly

- Result in a deep belief that the experience wasn't real

- Cause gut feelings that urge you to change your life, but with different themes and

ideas that come from desperation, not
from Divine guidance

• Have no sense of familiarity to it

• Feel forced, as if you're willing the experience or guidance to happen

Receiving Heaven's Messages as Thoughts

Your experiences with your angels may involve
ideas, revelations, or thoughts rather than your feelings. Many of the world's great thinkers and inventors get their innovative ideas from the ether. Here's
how to sort the true from the false:

A True Angelic Experience
Involving Thoughts

Such an encounter may:

• Involve concepts that are consistent and
repetitive

- Have a central theme of how you can help solve a problem or help others

- Be positive and empowering

- Give you explicit instructions about what step to take right now, and provide instructions for subsequent steps once you complete the first ones

- Bring exciting ideas that energize you

- Come out of the blue or in response to prayer

- Involve your taking human steps and doing some work

- Ring true and makes sense

- Be consistent with your natural interests, passions, or talents

- Let you know that a certain deceased loved one is near, without your seeing them

Imagination or False Guidance Involving Thoughts

Such an experience may:

- Be random and ever-changing

- Have a central theme of how you could get rich or famous

- Be discouraging and abusive

- Have you thinking about worst-case scenarios

- Consist of depressing or frightening thoughts

- Result in ideas coming slowly, in response to worry

- Be a get-rich-quick scheme

- Seem hollow and ill conceived

- Be unrelated to anything you've previously done or been interested in

- Have a primary motivation of desire to escape a current situation, rather than helping others

Hearing Heaven's Messages

It's a trite psychology-student joke that hearing voices is a sign of insanity. In contrast, many of the world's saints, sages, and great inventors have received guidance in this way. Prior to my carjacking experience, I heard a loud, clear voice warning me. And thousands of people have told me of receiving similar warnings that saved them or their loved ones from danger in ways that defy normal explanation.

The difference between hearing a true Divine voice, heeding the imagination, or having a hallucination is clear and distinct. I'll give you quite a bit of information about the variations between messages from your angels and your imagination. As for hallucinations, several scientists point out key distinctions:

- Researcher D. J. West gave this definition of the difference between a hallucination and a true psychic experience: "Pathological hallucinations tend to keep to certain rather rigid patterns, to occur repeatedly during a manifest illness but not at other times, and to be accompanied by other symptoms and particularly by disturbances of consciousness and loss of awareness of the normal surroundings. The spontaneous psychic [now often called "paranormal"] experience is more often an isolated event disconnected from any illness or known disturbance and definitely not accompanied by any loss of contact with normal surroundings."[1]

- Researcher Bruce Greyson, M.D., studied 68 people who were prescreened clinically to rule out schizophrenia. Dr. Greyson found that exactly half of these subjects reported having an apparition experience, where they had seen a deceased loved one with their physical eyes open.[2]

- Psychic researchers Karlis Osis, Ph.D., and Erlendur Haraldsson, Ph.D., noted that during most hallucinations, the people believe that they're seeing a living human being. During psychic experiences involving

visions, they believe that they're seeing
a celestial being, such as an angel, a
deceased loved one, or an ascended
master.[3]

Heaven may speak to us through a loud, disembodied voice outside our head; a quiet inner voice
inside our head; a conversation that we "happen" to
overhear; or by hearing music in our minds or over
and over again on the radio.

A True Angelic Experience
Involving Hearing

- Sentences usually begin with the words *you*
  or *we*.

- There's a sense that someone else is talking to you, even if it sounds like your own
  voice.

- It's readily apparent how the message
  relates to your immediate concerns or
  questions.

- The voice is to the point and blunt.

- The sound is loving and positive, even if it's warning you of danger.

- It asks you to take immediate action, including changing your thoughts or attitude to be more loving.

- You may hear a voice call your name upon awakening.

- You could be aware of strains of beautiful, disembodied "celestial" music.

- You might receive a message about self-improvement or helping others.

Imagination or False Guidance Involving Hearing

- Sentences usually begin with the word *I.*

- It feels like you're talking to yourself.

- The message is muddy, cryptic, or unclear.

- The voice is wordy and vague.

- It's taunting, alarming, or cruel.

- There's gossip and speculation about others.

- You hear abusive words.

- You experience loud, unpleasant noises or discordant music.

- There's a message to hurt yourself or others.

Seeing Heaven's Messages

Your angelic experiences may also involve what you see, either while awake, asleep, or meditating. There are many ways to sort the true visions from the false ones.

A True Angelic Experience
Involving Seeing

- Dream visitations almost seem surreal, with vivid colors and emotions.

- You see sparkles or flashes of light or colored mists.

- There's a feeling of spontaneity and naturalness to the vision.

- You experience repetitive instances of seeing a feather, coin, bird, butterfly, rainbow, number sequence, and so on, beyond chance occurrences.

- You receive service-oriented visions of yourself helping others.

Imagination or False Guidance
Involving Seeing

- Dreams seem ordinary and forgettable.

- You see worst-case scenarios without being given instructions on how to avoid them.

- You get the feeling that you're forcing the vision to occur.

- You look for a sign but find inconsistency or force the meaning that you want onto what you see.

- You receive an ego-centered vision of yourself gaining at the expense of others.

Paying Attention to the Messages

Whether your angelic messages come to you as a vision, a voice, an idea, a feeling, or a combination of these four elements, you can distinguish true from false guidance by paying attention to the characteristics in this chapter's lists. Be assured that if you're facing danger before it's your time to go, your angels will give you very loud and clear guidance, regardless of the form in which it appears. Information about daily life might appear more subtly, but in the following chapters, you'll read about ways to amplify its intensity and clarity.

Everyone has an equal ability to communicate with their angels, because all people are equally "gifted" spiritually. Some may appear to be more psychically adept than others; however, that's only because those individuals have been willing to listen, believe, and trust the input of their spiritual senses.

The single biggest block I find in my psychic-development students is that they try too hard to make an angelic experience happen. They want to see and hear an angel so desperately that they strain to do so. But anytime people grasp for something, they're coming from a place of fear. It could be the anxious thought *Maybe I won't be able to see or hear, Maybe I don't have angels,* or some other vague ego-based concern. The ego isn't psychic at all, being entirely fear based. Only the love-based Higher Self within each of us is able to communicate with the Divine.

So the more you can relax, the more easily you'll

be able to consciously commune with your angels. The breath is a wonderful starting place, as is optimism akin to what many children have. They say, "*Of course* I have angels. Everyone does!" Children don't care whether they're imagining their angelic visions; they simply enjoy and accept them. As a result, children easily see and hear their guardian angels. If you stopped worrying whether your Divine connection is real or not, you'd overcome the ego's blocks and enjoy your Higher Self's natural—and very real—gifts.

The angels say, *Fear is a natural predator of the psychic domain. It robs your psyche of its creative control and asks if you would allow it to dominate your moods, schedule, and decisions. It weakens you who are all-powerful. Your decision-making capability is impaired at its behest. Allow no terror to 'inter-fear' with your domain of happiness, for that is God's kingdom of great blessings. You're more powerful than any anxious force. Your Divine willingness can overcome any darkness that the world has ever seen. Your Creator's light will always blind any enemy if you will but focus on this radiance within your mind.*

So, instead of doubting our ability to connect with our angels, let's look at how we already do receive messages from Heaven and how we can enhance that connection even more. In the next few chapters, we'll look at ways to increase the volume and clarity of your angels' messages.

How to Feel Your Angels

When angels or deceased loved ones come extra close, you can feel their presence. Many people I interview can recall when they sensed a specific spirit nearby. Most say something such as "Yes, I could feel my mother with me the other night. It seemed so real, but I still wonder if I was just imagining it."

You may tend to discount your intuition and not trust yourself. How many times have you had a gut feeling to *not* get involved in a certain relationship, take a job, buy something, or drive a particular route? How often did you then override your feelings, do it anyway, and later regret it?

Of course, whether or not you listened to your inner guidance, such situations give you opportunities to learn to have faith and follow your Higher Self the next time. This is the process for communing with your angels and deceased loved ones—that is, it has to do with trusting that your feelings are a legitimate and accurate divining device, which God installed in you. In the case of discerning the presence of someone who's passed away, it involves trusting that you really can distinguish one person from another. In that way, everyone is a naturally gifted psychic medium.

Being a medium for strangers is done in the same feeling-based way that you can use for yourself. When I conduct a reading for someone I don't know, I first hold the intention of contacting that person's deceased loved ones. Most of my contact with the being is visual, because that's my basic channel of Divine communication, but a lot of my work is also feeling based.

After death, people still retain the energy patterns and physical dimensions of their former selves, and that's what a medium sees. Individuals who encounter apparitions of their deceased loved ones say that they look just the way they did when alive, only younger and more radiant. I've found that the energy patterns of those who have passed over are similar to wavelengths of the color spectrum: Older folks have slower and longer energy wavelengths, while young-sters have faster vibration, and females resonate more quickly than males.

It *is* possible to make contact solely by feeling, based on perceiving these sonarlike waves. Each person has a unique "fingerprint" to their personality, persona, behaviors, habits, and other distinguishing characteristics. Have you ever walked into your home and been able to feel who else was there—even though you lived with several people and had no physical evidence of their presence? Or, let's say that you're in the kitchen fixing a meal and you hear the front door open: Without using logic, perhaps you can detect who has arrived. Another example is when you go into a room full of people and can sense the mood of the crowd.

In the same way, when your deceased loved ones are close to you, they have unique energy fingerprints that you can feel. When I conduct mediumship sessions, I find that 90 percent of my clients already know which individuals are nearby—they're coming to me merely to validate their feelings. For some reason, they aren't willing to accept their intuition as valid until an outside "expert" confirms it.

You can imagine how difficult it must be for professional intuitives such as myself to stick their necks out and publicly hold these sessions on television, at workshops, and on radio programs. Most of the time when I'm doing so, I have no idea about the meaning of the information I'm relaying. Yet I trust my gut feelings enough to voice what I'm given, and most of the time my client will say, "Yes, that's exactly right!" It's taken me a lot of practice, a great deal of prayer, a brush with death, and many trials and errors to attain this level of confidence. My hope is that everyone will reach that state of trust in their emotional and physical feelings.

Common Ways in Which You Feel a Spiritual Presence

Here are some of the common ways you may connect with your angels and deceased loved ones through your feelings:

- Smelling their favorite cologne or other distinctive scent

- Catching a whiff of flowers or smoke when there's no blossom or fire nearby

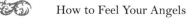

- Feeling that someone has touched you, stroked your hair, pushed you, protected you, tucked you in, or hugged you

- Perceiving someone sitting next to you, including seeing an indent on the sofa or bed where that deceased person or animal has just been

- Noticing an air-pressure change, a sense of tightness around your head, a feeling that something is pounding on your forehead, an impression of some spiritual essence moving through your head, or a sensation similar to being pulled underwater

You may also experience:

- Air-temperature changes

- A sudden surge of euphoria or bliss

- A gut feeling that this experience is surreal, even if you're reluctant to share it with others

- A sense of familiarity coming over you as
  a deceased person you knew well hovers
  nearby

True angelic experiences are warm, safe, loving, and comfortable, while false ones make you feel cold, prickly, and afraid. The inauthentic encounters can originate from the ego or from an Earthbound spirit. These beings are afraid to go to the Divine Light in the afterlife plane, either because they're attached to Earthly existence (possessions or addictions, for example) or because they're afraid of being judged by God and cast into "hell." So the entity stays near Earth and can interfere with a living person's happiness. More information on this subject can be found in my book *The Lightworker's Way* (Hay House, 1997).

A "touchy" subject (no pun intended) is that some Earthbound spirits will approach the living for sexual favors. I've met many widows and widowers who are comforted by having continued intimate relationships with their deceased husband or wife. But this is entirely different from the slew of New Age women I've recently encountered who report freely having sexual contact with nonphysical strangers in the spirit world. I consider these exchanges to be spiritually oppressive to the living, as a high-level guide or angel would never approach a human being for such favors. While the living women whom I've interviewed nearly always report a positive experience in these instances, the message I've strongly received is that these activities encourage low-level Earthbound entities to stay with us. They can also create barriers in entering into a new relationship, as potential suitors unconsciously sense the presence of another lover who's already on the scene.

Low-level encounters such as this will leave you feeling empty, while true contact reminds you that your angels and deceased loved ones are near you always. How do you tell if it's one of the latter who's helping you? An angel's energy will pull you upward in an indescribable way. You'll suddenly have a rush of love or joy without knowing why, or you'll get a strong gut feeling . . . and if you follow it, your life will grow in happy and miraculous ways. A deceased loved one will be distinctly familiar. You'll likely be able to identify the person, perhaps with an accompanying sensation of a hug, a touch, an air-pressure change, or a distinct aroma.

You can also use your feelings to "test-drive" an intuitive sensation and notice how you react. For instance, let's say that you're getting an urge to move to a new area. You're conflicted, however, wondering how such a change would affect your family, friends, and career. Even though some of these factors aren't clear to you, you can "try on your future" and get a better grip on your Divine guidance.

As you imagine what it would be like to stay living where you are, focus on your feelings. Is your heart full of relief, sadness, joy, or some other emotion? Does any part of your body tighten or relax in response to the mental image?

Now, compare your emotional and physical sensations when you imagine what it would be like to move. Your feelings are very accurate gauges of your soul's desires and your Divine will, which is one with God's will.

How to Increase Your Clairsentience

If you normally don't have a strong sense of your emotional or physical feelings, you can use the following methods to open this important channel of Heavenly communication. When you become more sensitive to your emotions and physical sensations, life becomes richer and relationships deepen; and you feel greater compassion and Divine love, understand others more readily, become more balanced, and are more apt to notice and follow your intuition.

Here are some steps that can increase your clairsentience:

— **Sleep next to clear quartz crystals.** You can purchase a clear quartz crystal "point" (a cylinder with a point at the end) fairly inexpensively at any metaphysical bookstore or gem show. Place the crystal in sunlight for at least four hours to clear away any psychic residue from its previous owner. Then, put one or more of these crystal points on your nightstand or beneath your bed. If they're on the nightstand, position the crystals on their sides, with the points facing your head. If the crystals are below your bed, have the points facing up, toward your head or your heart.

As you become more sensitive, you'll probably have to move the crystals so that their points face away from you. You may even need to reposition them farther from your bed. Highly sensitive clairsentients sometimes develop insomnia when crystals are too close to their sleeping area.

— **Work with the aroma of pink roses or rose essential oil.** The aroma of pink roses opens the heart chakra, which is the energy center that regulates clairsentience. Keep a pink rose nearby and breathe in its fragrance often, or purchase some high-quality essential oil made with real—not synthetic—rose. Put the oil over your heart, and dab some near your nose so that you can frequently enjoy its aroma.

— **Wear a rose quartz necklace.** Just as pink roses open the heart chakra, so does rose quartz crystal. This beautiful pink stone is attuned to the heart chakra. In addition to activating your clairsentience, rose quartz crystals can help you open up to romantic blessings in your life.

— **Increase your sensitivity to physical-touch exercises.** Close your eyes and handle an object on your desk. Touch it slowly and deliberately, noticing the minute details and textures. Rub the item along the back of your hand and your arm, and be aware of the sensations. Have a trusted friend gently blindfold you and hand you unknown items to touch or food samples to taste. Put all of your awareness on your physical and emotional sensations, and try to guess what each thing is.

— **Tune up your body with cardiovascular exercise and light eating.** When you feel tired, heavy, or sluggish, it's more difficult to discern your feelings. Jogging, brisk walking, yoga, or other cardiovascular exercise helps you more precisely pinpoint the meaning and messages behind your clairsentience. Similarly, eating light, healthful foods keeps you from being weighed down. A sense of heaviness or being stuffed from food can block your awareness of Divine guidance. Anything that can make your body feel better—including massage, a nap, or a bubble bath—will heighten your sensitivity to your gut feelings.

Protecting Yourself

Clairsentients often complain that they're *too* sensitive. "I absorb the toxic energy of other people's problems," and "I get overwhelmed because I can feel everyone else's emotions," are the two chief complaints among the feeling-oriented set.

Ironically, clairsentients often enter professions that increase their likelihood of physical contact with others. Massage, energy healing, medicine, and counseling are a few common occupations among people who understand the world through their feelings. And while feeling-oriented individuals are excellent at those professions, they must take measures to ensure that they don't absorb residue from their clients' negative emotions.

There are two ways to deal with this issue: preventive measures and clearing activities. Preventive measures involve shielding yourself from others' toxic energies. Clearing activities entail releasing any such energies that you *do* absorb, including those that stem from your own fearful thoughts.

Shielding

Preventive measures are a little like birth control—they're not 100 percent effective, but they do provide considerable protection. There are dozens of ways to shield yourself, and I'm just including my two favorites.

1. Music: The angels say that music acts as a psychic screen, surrounding us with protective energy. In stressful situations, then, it's a good idea to have music continually playing around us.

Music is not only a preventive measure; it's also a clearing measure. Archangel Sandalphon is the angel of music, and he works with Archangel Michael to clear away the effects of negative energy. Call upon

Sandalphon to help you select the best music for various situations. Have a CD playing when you meditate, and ask Sandalphon to work with the melody to shield and clear you.

2. Pink light: The angels taught me this method one day when I was at the gym. I said hello to a woman I'd never met before whose path crossed mine on the free-weights floor. She began telling me about her numerous medical operations in minute detail. I knew that she needed to express herself and wanted a friendly ear. However, I also was aware that she was spewing out toxic energy with her endless discourse on illness and disease.

I mentally called upon my angels for help. *Surround yourself with a tube of pink light,* they immediately counseled me. I envisioned myself encircled by a tall cylinder of pink illumination, as if I were inside a lipstick tube. It extended above my head and below my feet.

You've never liked shielding yourself with white light, the angels reminded me, *because you felt as if you were cutting yourself off from others. Since your life's mission specifically calls for you to interact with people and not isolate yourself (as you did in your most recent past life), you have shied away from using the white-light shield.*

Their words were true. Although I knew all about shielding methods, I rarely used them because I wanted to be there for my clients. I'd once worked with a psychiatrist who counseled people from behind a gigantic oak desk. I'd always thought that he used it as a buffer to avoid emotional intimacy with his patients—it was also a power symbol. I didn't want to employ white light during my counseling sessions, because it felt like I was isolating myself from my clients.

The angels reminded me, *But notice how this pink shield of light is very different. See how it radiates intense Divine love energy out toward this woman. Notice, also, how it projects beautifully strong Heavenly energy inward toward yourself. And nothing can permeate this pink-light shield but energies that originate from Divine love. So, in this way, you can be fully present for this woman, without taking her illusions of suffering upon yourself.*

Since that day, I've been using the pink-shield technique with great results—and positive feedback from those I've taught it to. Thank you, angels!

Clearing

We sometimes feel tired, irritable, or depressed without knowing why. Often the culprit stems from our contact with other people's negative mind-sets. If you work in a helping profession, your exposure to toxic emotions is especially high, and it's essential to clear these energies from yourself regularly.

Here are my three favorite clearing methods:

1. Plants: Probably the simplest way to clear yourself of psychic debris is with the help of Mother Nature. Just as plants convert carbon dioxide into fresh oxygen, they also transmute lower energies. Greenery is especially helpful in ridding our bodies of energetic toxins.

The angels urge us all to keep a plant next to our bed—a potted one on the nightstand can do wonders while you sleep! It absorbs the heavy energy that you've ingested during the day and sends it into the ethers. Don't worry . . . it won't harm the plant.

If you work with people in any way, but especially as a massage therapist or counselor (where you're open to receiving your clients' released negativity), place plants near your workstation. You'll feel more refreshed at the end of the day by taking this one simple step! The angels say that broad-leafed plants work best, because the wide leaves absorb greater energy fields. So a pothos or philodendron would be a good choice. Avoid prickly or pointy leaves in the plants that surround you. Interestingly, feng shui, the ancient Chinese art of placement, also recommends staying away from pointy-leafed varieties. Apparently, their swordlike leaves don't promote positive energy flow.

2. Etheric cord cutting: Anyone who works with other people, either professionally or by offering unpaid acts of kindness, should know about etheric cords and how to handle them. Basically, whenever a person forms a fear-based attachment to you (such as being afraid that you'll leave them, or believing that you are their source of energy or happiness), a cord is constructed between the two of you. This tie is visible to anyone who is clairvoyant, and palpable to anyone who is intuitive.

The cords resemble surgical tubing, and they function like gasoline hoses. When a needy person has formed an attachment to you, that person suctions energy from you through this etheric cord. You may not see it, but you can feel its effect: namely, feeling tired or sad without knowing why. Well, it's because the person at the other end has just drawn on your power or sent you toxic energy through the cord.

So anytime you've helped someone—or whenever you feel lethargic, sad, or tired—it's a good idea to "cut your cords." You aren't rejecting, abandoning, or divorcing the person by cutting these bonds. You're only severing the dysfunctional, fearful, codependent area of the relationship. The loving part of it remains attached.

To cut your own cords, say either mentally or aloud:

> *"Archangel Michael, I call upon
> you now. Please cut the cords of
> fear that are draining my energy
> and vitality. Thank you."*

Then be silent for a few moments. Be sure to inhale and exhale deeply during the process, as breath opens the door for angels to help you. You'll probably feel cords being cut or pulled out of you. You may sense air-pressure changes or other tangible signs that the cord cutting is occurring.

The people on the other end will think of you without knowing why at the moment that their cord is being cut. You may even find that you get lots of "just thinking about you" phone messages and e-mails from those you were "attached" to. Don't buy into faulty beliefs about these people. Remember, *you* are not their source of energy or happiness—God is. The cords will grow back each time a person forms a fear-based attachment to you, so keep cutting them as needed.

3. Vacuuming: When we worry about someone, blame ourselves for a person's misery, or massage someone who's in emotional pain, we may take on their negative psychic energy in a misguided form of helpfulness. Everyone does this, especially lightworkers who are ultra-concerned about aiding others—often at their own expense. The angels give us methods such as this one to help us stay balanced in our service work. They want us to help people, but not to hurt ourselves in the process. It's a matter of being open to receiving support from others, including the angels. Many lightworkers are wonderful at giving aid, but not so good at receiving it. This is a method to help counterbalance that tendency.

To vacuum yourself with the help of the angels, mentally say, *"Archangel Michael, I call upon you now to clear and vacuum the effects of fear."* You'll then mentally see or feel a large being appear—this is Archangel

Michael. He will be accompanied by smaller angels known as the "Band of Mercy."

Notice that Michael is holding a vacuum tube. Watch as he puts it in through the top of your head (known as the "crown chakra"). You must decide whether you want the vacuum speed to be on extra-high, high, medium, or low. You'll also be directing him where to put the tube during the clearing process. Mentally direct it inside your head, in your body, and around all of your organs. Vacuum every part, all the way to the tips of your fingers and toes.

You may see or feel clumps of psychic dirt go through the vacuum tube, just like when you're cleaning a dirty carpet. Any entities that enter the vacuum are humanely treated at the other end by the Band of Mercy, who meets and escorts entities to the Light. Keep vacuuming until no more psychic debris goes through the tube.

As soon as you're clear, Archangel Michael will reverse the switch so that thick, toothpaste-like white light comes out of the tube. This is a form of "caulking" material that will fill in the spaces that formerly held psychic dirt.

Vacuuming is one of the most powerful techniques I've ever tried. You can also use this method on others, in person or remotely. Just hold the intention of working on them, and it's done. Even if you don't clearly see or feel anything during the process, or you worry *Am I just making this up?* the results will be palpable. Most people see an immediate lifting of depression and a cessation of anger following a vacuuming session.

Being in Touch with Your Feelings

With practice, you become increasingly tuned in to your feelings and are more apt to trust their wisdom. If you add to your spiritual repertoire with the power of your thoughts and ideas, you'll have two clear avenues to receive and follow your Divine guidance. In the next chapter, we'll examine the power of claircognizance, or thoughts from Heaven.

How to Recognize and Receive Divine Ideas and Profound Thoughts

When there's some tidbit of knowledge that you know for sure, without knowing *how* you know, it's called *claircognizance,* or "clear knowing." Maybe this has happened to you: You're arguing with a person about a topic that you're only vaguely familiar with, but something deep inside of you tells you a fact or two, and you cling to this knowledge without having evidence to support it. Your companion asks, "But *how* do you know?" And you have no retort but to say, "I just know—that's all."

You've probably been called a "know-it-all" a few times in your life, and this proclamation has a grain of truth to it. You *do* know a lot, but you're totally puzzled about how you came to own all this information.

Many great inventors, scientists, authors, futurists, and leaders have used their gift of claircognizance to tap into the collective unconscious and access new ideas and inspiration. Thomas Edison, for instance, said, "All progress, all success, springs from thinking." It's said that Edison and other great inventors meditated until they received a brainstorm of inspiration and ideas.

The difference between someone who simply receives such information and a person who also benefits from it is the ability to accept what's happening as being useful and special. So many claircognizants write off their incoming transmissions as information that's glaringly obvious to others. *Everyone knows this stuff,* claircognizants will say to themselves. Then, two years later, they find that the brilliant idea they'd conceived has been carried out and marketed by another person. So, the challenge for those who receive their Divine guidance as a thought, idea, or revelation is to accept that this is a unique piece of information that *really could be the answer to their prayer.*

Let's say that you've been praying for Divine guidance to help you leave your job and become self-employed. You then receive an idea for a business that would help others, and this thought comes to you again and again (two characteristics of true Divine guidance). Will you discount it, thinking, *Well, everyone dreams of self-employment, so obviously this is pie-in-the-sky wishful thinking?*

I've found that claircognizants benefit from spending time away from the computer and office by getting a healthy dose of nature and fresh air. Many thinking-oriented people lead work-centered lives, creating a need for balance in the areas of physical fitness, playfulness, family matters, spirituality, and relationships. Even focusing a little extra time on these things can help a claircognizant feel clearer in following ideas that are born of the Infinite Mind.

Judgment vs. Discernment

Those who favor a "thinking" style with regard to angelic communication may have higher intelligence quotients (IQs) than most. After all, they're usually avid readers, with a wide range of interests that would land them higher-than-average IQ scores.

A key ingredient in tapping into that intellectual awareness is being able to differentiate between when you're using discernment versus when you're relying on judgment. There are key differences between these two intellectual behaviors that can determine spiritual outcomes.

Let's start with an example involving cigarette smoking. You're probably aware of the many studies linking this habit to various diseases and health risks. Discernment would say, "I'm not attracted to smoking or smokers. I don't care for the smell of cigarettes or their effects." Judgment would say, "Smoking is bad. Smokers are bad." Notice the difference? One operates under the "Law of Attraction," which simply asks you to honor your personal preferences without labeling or condemnation.

In a similar vein, when you're unsure whether or not an idea is Divinely guided, pay attention to your internal mechanisms of discernment. The old adage "If in doubt, don't" has a lot of wisdom to it. Your inner computer knows if something is off or not. You might not need to reject an entire idea, but you may have to rethink or revise certain components of it.

You may need to seek out specialists in areas that are outside of your expertise. If this is the case, mentally ask God and your angels to lead you to these individuals, and you'll delight in seeing how quickly they come to you.

I experienced this phenomenon when I felt that I was supposed to write a book on vegetarianism. I knew that I needed to find a collaborator who was a registered dietitian with a spiritual bent—one who was also familiar with vegetarianism. With full faith, I turned my request to find such a person over to God. Three weeks later, at one of my workshops a registered dietitian named Becky Prelitz introduced herself to me. She had come to see me speak because she was very immersed in spiritual teaching and living. *This is the woman I'm looking for!* I thought. The more I talked to Becky, the more convinced I became that she was the expert who was the answer to my prayer. Today, Becky and her husband, Christopher, are great friends of my husband, Steven, and me; and our book, *Eating in the Light: Making the Switch to Vegetarianism on Your Spiritual Path,* was published by Hay House in 2001.

Common Ways in Which Claircognizance Occurs

Here are some of the ways in which you may have already received Divine communication through your thought processes:

- You met a new person and suddenly knew details about him or her without having had previous knowledge of the individual.

- You possessed information about something related to current events without having read or heard about it.

- You had a premonition of how something (a business venture, a recreational trip, or a relationship, for example) was going to turn out . . . and you were right.

- You had an idea for a business, a book, or an invention that haunted you. You executed the idea and found that it worked out favorably. Or, you ignored it and discovered that someone else with the same idea ran with it and made a fortune.

- You lost your checkbook, keys, or wallet, and when you asked your angels where the item was, you received a sudden knowingness that led you right to it.

True Divine claircognizance is repetitive and positive. It speaks of ways in which you can improve your own life and the lives of others. It's service oriented, and while a certain idea may make you rich and famous, that's a side benefit and *not* the motivation behind the concept. In fact, it's usually these types of altruistic ideas that lead to benefits for their inventors. Those who pursue self-serving ventures often repel potential clients and customers, who sense the hollow values behind an idea. My publisher and mentor, Louise L. Hay, once told me that her financial life finally healed when she began focusing on how she could serve, rather than on what she could get. When I applied this same principle to my own life, I found that it had remarkably curative effects on my level of happiness, as well as on my career and income.

True claircognizance helps you do something that will truly help others, in such a way that it will inspire people to seek you out as customers, clients, sponsors, audience members, publishers, and so forth. This force comes from the Creator, Who knows of your true talents, passions, and interests, and how these characteristics can be used to help others. In biblical times, money was referred to as "talents," and *you* have talents that you can exchange for money.

True claircognizance doesn't just wave a dream under our noses and then taunt us to discover how to manifest it. No! It gives us complete, step-by-step instructions. The trick, though, is to remember that God only teaches us one step at a time. We receive this information in the form of repetitive thoughts (or feelings, visions, or words, depending upon our spiritual orientation) that tell us to *do something*. The "something" usually seems insignificant: Call this person, write this letter, attend this meeting, read this book, for example. If we follow the directions and complete Step A, then in the same repetitive manner, we're given the next set of instructions for Step B. Step-by-step, God guides us all the way to the realization of our intended manifestation.

We always have free will, so we can ignore the guidance anytime we choose. However, most people find that if they don't complete one of the Divinely guided steps, they feel stuck, as if they're spinning their wheels in the mud. I always ask people who tell me that they feel blocked, "What piece of Divine guidance have you been repetitively receiving but are ignoring?" Always, I find that this insight (which they're avoiding because of some fear of making a life change) is the key ingredient they've been searching for.

Angels give you ideas in response to your prayers for guidance. You receive this Divine transmission at moments when your mind is receptive, such as during dream time, meditation, exercise, or even while watching a television program or movie (when your mind tends to go on cruise control). You'll feel excited and energized by Divinely guided insights, and it's important not to counteract them with pessimistic thoughts. The idea rings true, and you'll know—deep in your soul—that this is it! Certainly, any idea can fail. *But it can also succeed!* And trying is what gives your life meaning at the end of the day.

If you've had some negative experiences with respect to following hunches in the past, you could understandably feel gun-shy now. You may have decided to play it safe and secure by avoiding major life changes. That's fine, as long as you're happy with your current circumstances! But if there's an area of your life that's off balance, it's natural for you (as well as God and the angels) to want to heal the situation. That's called achieving "homeostasis," which is the instinctive drive to attain balance that's common to all living things.

Skepticism, Pragmatism, and Faith

More than the other Divine guidance styles, clair-cognizants tend to waver when it comes to faith. When you're a thinker, it's easy to think yourself into a box of skepticism. Faith seems illogical and rests upon so many intangible factors.

Yet a good scientist always experiments before drawing a conclusion. Whether your hypothesis is geared in favor of believing in angels or not, take the time to put the theory to a test. For instance, God and the angels hear your thoughts (don't worry—they don't judge them), so you can call upon Heaven without eliciting raised eyebrows from your colleagues.

Mentally ask your angels to help you with some area of your personal or professional life. Then, notice what help comes to you after you've made your request. It could be an instant response, where you have a strong impulse or idea, or it may come in a more tangible fashion, where a person will "just happen" to hand you a journal article with the information you seek. The two key ingredients in this experiment are: (1) *asking* for guidance (the Law of Free Will prevents Heaven from helping without our giving permission), and (2) *noticing* the help that's being received.

Being aware of this type of assistance is entirely different from holding a forced scavenger hunt where you're searching for clues. False guidance is always the product of struggle and worry. True Divine inspiration comes easily on natural wings of love.

I find that most claircognizant people have had experiences with their deceased loved ones in which they knew that their grandparent, their parent, or another beloved person was with them. Without actually seeing or feeling that deceased individual's presence, the claircognizant had a *knowingness* of the loved one's proximity. This same sort of knowingness creates other psychic hits for claircognizants in their careers, family, and health. Without being aware of how they know, claircognizants receive incoming information that's both accurate and helpful.

The more you can learn to trust and follow such information, the more you'll benefit from your internal guidance system. For instance, you may get an idea about opening a new business. The idea is foolproof, and you wonder why you never thought of it before. You venture forward, and all the doors open for you: financing, location, partnerships, and more. The business is a rapid success, and you know that you were guided by true Divine wisdom.

The Spiritual Mentorship Program

There are many beings in Heaven who'd like to help you, and not all of them are your guardian angels. Some are ordinary people who've passed on and who have a strong desire to teach and help those of us still living. Many of these people are extremely talented and accomplished, and they form what's known as the "Spiritual Mentorship Program."

On Earth a mentor is an accomplished person in your chosen field who shows you the ropes and gives you advice, guidance, and introductions. The Spiritual Mentorship Program is similar, in that you're assigned to an expert who spends time guiding you through the process related to your chosen vocation or avocation.

You can work with a famous deceased person or any unknown-but-great individual in the spirit world. Most are very happy to pass along their knowledge. It gives them a sense of meaning to help others, in the same way that you enjoy performing service work. And there's no charge for their services, so you can meet with them in your own home—wearing your pajamas!

When I first felt guided to contact a mentor, I chose a specific author whom I greatly admire (he won't allow me to divulge his name because he feels that would only give glory to his ego-personality). So I mentally asked him to help me write the book *The Lightworker's Way.* Immediately, he came to me.

Although I could only faintly see him, I sensed his presence on a feeling, knowing, and hearing level quite strongly.

I was so surprised that this author actually came to visit me (I was starstruck!) that I didn't know what to say. I stammered, "You . . . you . . . you're here!"

The author then said to me, "You're obviously not ready. Please call me when you're better prepared to work with me."

At that time, I was just beginning to give psychic readings to famous people whom I highly respected. I noticed that my admiration of their work made me feel intimidated by them. I'd act differently around these celebrities from the way I'd behave around "regular" people. This bugged me, because I knew this was an ego issue. It meant that I saw famous people as being "above" me—or, in other words, as being separated from me.

Therefore, I asked Jesus and the archangels to come into my dreams and clear away any ego issues that made me think anyone was either above me or below me. As always, this request worked immediately! In the morning, I felt a shift. I can't explain *how* it happened. I can just tell you that it *did* happen. From that point forward, I didn't feel intimidated by people whom I admired.

Since that time, I've called upon additional mentors to help me. One time I was jogging and experienced terrible pain in the side of my stomach (known as a "stitch"). I immediately asked for help and was pleasantly surprised when a man in the spirit world came to me whom I recognized as Jim Fixx, the late author of *The Complete Book of Running.* He told me to concentrate on keeping the top of my head level, instead of using my bouncy head-bobbing running style. This meant extending the length and smoothness of each stride. When I stopped bouncing my head up and down, my side stitches went away, and I haven't had any recurrences. Jim also helps me with endurance and speed while running.

I've taught many audience members about the Spiritual Mentorship Program, and the majority of them have successfully "adopted" a mentor in Heaven. Some of these mentors are famous inventors, writers, healers, and musicians who've passed on. For instance, a premed student in Chicago writes letters to Albert Einstein and receives guidance, a songwriter in Atlanta corresponds with John Denver using automatic writing, and an architect in the Midwest talks with Michelangelo for inspiration.

To engage in the Spiritual Mentorship Program, simply think about a being with whom you'd like to correspond. If you can't come up with anyone specific, ask God and the angels to assign a person to you who's an expert in a particular area (just as I did when I was running).

Then, even if you can't hear, see, or feel the presence of your new mentor, ask the person a question anyway. Either write this query down on paper, type it on a computer or typewriter, think it, or say it aloud. The mentor will hear your question, regardless of how you ask it.

Notice the answers that come to you as thoughts, words, feelings, or visions. It's a good idea to write the questions and answers down, like in an interview. (A full explanation of how to engage in "automatic writing" is on page 160.)

Whether you believe that these messages from your spiritual mentors are literal or figurative, you'll find that writing down your questions, and then recording the answers that you receive as thoughts, words, feelings, or visions, opens you up to new ideas and creative insights.

How to Increase Your Claircognizance

Since claircognizance can come about subtly, as a thought or an idea, it's easy to miss this high-level method by which Heaven communicates with us. You might dismiss your Divinely inspired idea without recognizing it as an answer to your prayers. You could mistake it for an idle thought or a daydream, instead of Heaven's inspiration.

Claircognizants also ignore their Divine guidance because they believe that what they know is obvious to others. "Everybody knows that!" a claircognizant will decide, and won't capitalize on the brilliant idea that they just received. It doesn't help that many claircognizants have been teased for being know-it-alls, so they hesitate to speak up for fear of being ridiculed. Yet this label has a kernel of truth to it, for claircognizants are very tapped into the collective unconscious.

So, it's important to really pay attention to what enters your mind . . . that includes the repetitive thoughts and also the novel ideas. Divine guidance comes both as suggestions that hammer away at you repeatedly and also as lightbulb-type inspirations. One of the best ways to pay attention to this form of guidance is to keep a daily journal where you have a conversation with yourself about your thoughts and ideas. The journal format could be like an interview with your Higher Self, perhaps set up in a question-and-answer format. In this way, you can more easily bring unconscious information to your awareness.

When you get a response, don't second-guess yourself. Instead, give your thoughts and ideas a moment to speak up. Ask them, "What do you want to tell me?" It could be an insight such as "This new person I've just been introduced to doesn't seem honorable." Or it could be an inspired idea that helps you *know* the truth of a spiritual principle, or a walloping brainstorm for a can't-miss new business.

By keeping a journal, you can assess the patterns and accuracy of your thoughts and ideas. You'll get in the habit of gaining awareness about which ones are truly Divinely inspired. You've probably had the experience of ignoring your thoughts and saying later, "I *knew* that was going to happen!" or "I *knew* I shouldn't have gone there!" Your successes and mistakes teach you both to trust and follow your insights.

I also find that many people who are thinking oriented (as opposed to feeling, sight, or hearing oriented) tend to be workaholics. They often hole up in their offices, strapped to the chairs in front of their computers. All this work is fine, as long as it's balanced with time spent outdoors. Yet I usually have to urge claircognizants to go out in nature. It's foreign to their comfort zones! Once outside, though, claircognizants find that the fresh air, plants, and trees help sharpen their psychic senses. They become even more open to, and aware of, their Divine inspiration.

The peace of the outdoors makes it easier to hear our thoughts and take note of clever ideas. As we clear room in our schedule for personal time-outs, we take a break from the world of clocks and telephones. We become more tuned in to the inner rhythm of our bodies—and all of nature. Among other benefits, spending regular time outdoors helps us develop "good timing," which really means that we notice and follow the rhythm of life. When we return to the office, we've developed more acute instincts with respect to the best moment to make that phone call, send that e-mail, or speak up at that meeting. Our time outdoors might also inspire us to break away from the office completely and forge a career that matches our heart's desire more fully.

True and False Claircognizance

Some people are skeptical about following their intuition because they've done so in the past and have been burned as a result. Perhaps you had a great idea one time, but when you followed through on it, everything turned into a mess, so you're reluctant to ever trust your ideas again.

Usually, these situations involve two types of patterns:

1. Our initial idea was Divinely inspired, but then fear took us off the path. When we initially received the idea, it was based upon true Divine guidance, which always stems from love. But somewhere along the way, we got scared. This fear blocked our receptivity to continued guidance and creative ideas, took us off our original inspired path, and triggered behavior and decisions that originated from the ego. When we partner with our egos, unhappiness and errors inevitably follow.

For instance, a woman I know named Bernice had a wonderful idea to start a home-based business as a personal fitness trainer. The idea seemed perfect, as it was a service that would help others in a field that she enjoyed, and it would allow her to stay home with her toddler while earning some money. So Bernice quit her day job and opened the business at her home. The first month, five people signed up as clients, which provided Bernice with enough money to pay her bills plus have extra money left over.

Yet Bernice worried whether her initial success would continue. *Where will my new clients come from?* she fretted. After ruminating on her future for a few days, Bernice decided to purchase advertising in several newspapers. She also bought full-color brochures, with matching stationery and business cards. Her expenses for these investments were high, but Bernice decided that she needed to "spend money to make money."

The next month, Bernice only signed up one new client. She worried even more about her business and spent additional money on advertising. But nothing that she tried seemed to work, and within four months, Bernice decided to return to her previous job to ensure that she'd bring in a steady income.

What happened? she wondered. In reviewing her situation, we find that Bernice truly did receive Divine guidance in starting her business. This was reinforced by her initial success, which gave her enough money to pay her bills, with a surplus afterward. It was only when Bernice began to let fear creep into the picture that things started to dry up. That's also when she started forcing things to happen through misguided advertising and unnecessary purchases. Her expenses went up and her income went down because she began listening to her ego's fears rather than her Higher Self's reassurance and guidance.

2. Instead of acknowledging our Divine guidance, we forced something to happen, or we

listened to another person's opinion and ignored our inner teacher. Sometimes we want to hear what we want to hear, so we'll decide that "he's the guy," even if our intuition (and best friends) are screaming that he's a creep. Or, we'll decide that God wants us to quit our job and move to Sedona, Arizona, when our gut feelings urge us to make a gradual career transition. In some cases, we'll betray our intuition and do something that's against our better judgment, because a strong-willed person talks us into it.

True and False Claircognizant Guidance

So, how *do* you know if an idea is God-inspired brilliance or a route to a wild-goose chase? Chapter 4 lists distinctions between true and false guidance. With regard to thoughts, ideas, and revelations, the characteristics to notice are:

— **Consistency.** True guidance is repetitive, and the idea will stick with you over time. Although it may build in detail and application, the core notion will stay the same. False guidance changes its course and structure constantly.

— **Motivation.** True guidance is motivated by a desire to improve a situation. False guidance's chief aim is to make you rich and famous. Although true guidance may yield those rewards, they are side benefits and not the central motivation for the idea.

— **Tone.** True guidance is uplifting, motivating, and encouraging. It urges you on, saying, "You can do it!" False guidance is the opposite, shredding your confidence to pieces.

— **Origination.** True guidance appears quickly, like a lightning bolt, in response to prayer or meditation. False guidance comes slowly, in response to worry. When you get an idea, back up and examine the trail of thoughts preceding it. If you were worrying about something, your ego may have conjured up a scheme to rescue you. If you were meditating peacefully, however, your Higher Self had the room to truly connect with the Divine collective unconscious and has probably handed you a gem of an idea.

— **Familiarity.** An idea that comes from true Divine guidance generally fits in with your natural inclinations, talents, passions, and interests. False guidance usually contains "left field" advice involving activities that hold no interest for you.

By noticing these characteristics, you can increase your faith in the ideas that you follow. You'll know that you're on the right path, and you'll use all of your higher intentions to create success. A healthy confidence level correlates to holding clear, laser-focused thoughts that lead to rapid manifestation.

If you combine your claircognizance with the ability to hear the voice of the Divine, as we'll discuss in the next section, you'll take your idea-manufacturing process to an even higher level.

Chapter Seven

How to Hear Your Angels

I think it's ironic that I, a former psychotherapist who once worked in locked hospital psychiatric wards, now teach people how to hear voices! Yet, when we listen for the voice of God and the angels, it's the sanest sound we'll ever hear. It can show us love in the face of seeming chaos and provide us with logical solutions when challenges arise.

Hearing the voice of Spirit is called *clairaudience,* or "clear hearing." In this chapter, we'll discuss what it is, and how to increase its volume and clarity.

Common Ways in Which
You Hear Heaven's Voice

Chances are excellent that you've heard your angels and other spiritual beings speak to you throughout your life. Have any of the following situations happened to you?

- Upon awakening, you hear your name called by a disembodied voice.

- Out of nowhere, you detect a strain of beautiful, celestial-sounding music.

- You hear a song repeatedly, either in your head or on the radio.

- There's a loud, shrill ringing noise in one ear.

- You overhear a conversation in which a stranger says the exact thing that you need to hear.

- You just "happen" to turn on the television or radio at the precise moment when a relevant discussion is occurring.

- You hear a deceased loved one's voice in your mind, in a dream, or outside of your head.

- You pick up on a living loved one's call for help, and it turns out that he or she needed assistance just then.

- A telephone or doorbell rings—no one is there, but you can sense that your deceased loved one is trying to get your attention.

- A disembodied voice gives you a warning or a life-enhancing message.

- You're looking for a lost item, you pray for assistance, and then you hear a voice tell you where to locate it.

Answers Come in Response to Questions

God and the angels speak to us in response to our queries, so we can kick-start a conversation simply by directing a question to them.

One time I wanted to know why certain Christian factions promoted the idea that it was beneficial to "fear God." I just couldn't understand why anyone would be afraid of our loving Creator, nor why a person would *aspire* to fear Him. So I asked my angels to help me understand this belief system. No sooner had I posed the question than I was scanning the radio stations in my car and the scanner stopped on a Christian talk show. At that very moment, the host began explaining why Christians "should" fear God. I didn't agree with his message, but I was very grateful to receive the answer to my question . . . especially so quickly after asking.

Is there a question that you have or some area of your life in which you desire guidance? Take a moment right now and mentally ask God and the angels about it. Hold the intention of giving that question to Heaven, and trust that you'll receive an answer. Even if you can't hear any Divine beings answering you right now, be assured that they can definitely hear you!

You should receive an auditory response to your question within a day or so. Sometimes you'll hear the answer in the form of a song. You may notice a tune playing repeatedly on the radio or in your mind. The answer to your question might be in the lyrics. Or, if the song reminds you of someone, it could be a message that this person (living or deceased) is thinking about you.

Usually when we hear a voice call out in the morning, it means that our angels or guides simply want to say hello to us. It's easiest for them to deliver this greeting when we're just waking up because our lucid mind is more open to spiritual communications. We're also more apt to remember the message when half-awake, as opposed to being fully asleep. If they have another revelation to add to their greeting, they'll specify that message to us at the same time. So when you hear your name called, don't worry that someone wants to get through to you. It's simply a loving greeting to let you know that you're being watched over.

If, after asking Heaven a question, you don't receive a reply, it could be that you've overlooked it. Or maybe you don't want to hear the information that Heaven is sending you because you didn't appreciate the guidance you were given at some time in the past. Thus, you block yourself from picking up on it. Keep repeating the question until you obtain the answer. Ask your angels to help you hear, and it will happen eventually.

A spiritual-counseling student of mine named Tienna was frustrated because she'd been in my psychic-development course for three days and still hadn't heard from her angels. Tienna complained that during her angel readings, she only heard staccato—one- or two-word messages. For instance, she was giving a reading to a classmate and heard the words *uncle* and *car accident* in her ear. Well, it turned out that Tienna's classmate had lost an uncle in a car accident.

"But I want to hear more than just one or two words!" Tienna complained. "I want to have full-on conversations with God and the angels."

I asked Tienna's angels for help, and I heard them say to her, *Just stay in the class, Tienna. With persistence and patience, you will hear us soon.* I relayed that message to Tienna.

By the fifth day of our spiritual-counseling class, Tienna bounded up to me excitedly. "I hear them, I hear them!" she exclaimed. She had a clairaudient breakthrough in exactly the way that her angels had predicted: through persistent intention to hear, and through patience in surrendering "when" that would happen. From that day forward, Tienna had full-blown auditory discussions with her angels, who gave her both personal guidance and information for her clients.

Ringing in the Ears

Many lightworkers report hearing a high-pitched ringing sound in one ear. It's a shrill noise that can be painful and intrusive. When checked by a physician, tinnitus (a disturbance of the auditory nerve) is usually ruled out. That's because the ringing is of a nonphysical origin. It's a band of woven information, encoded in electrical impulses. Heaven downloads guidance, assistance, and information through this bandwidth, which sounds like a computer modem hooking into the Internet.

Sometimes the ringing is accompanied by a pinching or pulling sensation on the earlobe. This happens when the angels and guides especially want your attention. You don't need to consciously understand the message encoded within the ringing sound—you just need to commit to receiving it. The information will be stored in your unconscious, where it will positively influence your actions, ensuring that you don't procrastinate with respect to your lightworker mission.

Please don't worry that the ringing could be coming from a lower or dark source. The sound shows that the energetic frequency of the encoded information originates from a high place of Divine love.

Lower forces wouldn't be able to work with such an elevated frequency.

The ringing sound is actually an answer to your prayers for guidance about your life's mission. If it becomes too loud, painful, or intrusive, mentally tell your angels that it's hurting you, and ask them to turn down the volume. The information will still be transmitted to you; it will just come to you in a quieter fashion. If the earlobe pinching or pulling becomes painful, tell your angels and guides about the discomfort, and ask them to stop.

When I asked my angels and guides to turn down the volume of the ringing and to stop hurting me with earlobe pinching, I was never again bothered by loud tones or painful ears. The angels certainly aren't offended by our requests. They need our feedback so that they best know how to help us.

How Do I Know Who's Talking to Me?

If you're concerned about the true identity of a voice that's speaking to you, simply ask your "caller" to identify him- or herself. If you don't believe or trust the answer that you receive, ask the spiritual being to prove his or her identity to you. As you'll discover, the entity will say or do something that will stir beautiful emotions within you or will be something that only that particular being could do or say. Here are some guidelines:

- God's voice sounds very loud, to the point, friendly, and casual, with good humor and modern vernacular.

- The archangels are very loud, to the point, formal, and direct. They speak a lot about Divine love; getting on track with our mission; and overcoming doubts, fears, and procrastination with respect to it.

- The angels sound almost Shakespearean at times, with very archaic and formal speech patterns.

- Our deceased loved ones sound just as they did when they were living, although their voice may seem stronger and younger. They'll use the same vocabulary and speaking style that they did when they were physically alive.

- Our Higher Self sounds like our own voice.

- The ego comes across as abusive, discouraging, paranoid, and depressing; and it begins sentences with the word *I* because it's egocentric.

How to Increase Your Clairaudience

We're all naturally psychic, and this ability includes clairaudience and all of the other "clairs." We usually find, however, that each person possesses one primary channel of Divine communication. Some people are naturally auditory, and the first thing they observe when they meet someone new is the sound of that person's voice. Others are naturally visual, and the first thing they notice in a new acquaintance is that person's appearance, including his or her movements and actions. Those who are naturally feeling oriented note how new people make them feel, if they touch them, and even how the fabric of their clothing feels. Thinking-oriented individuals are aware of whether a new person is interesting, intelligent, potentially helpful in their career, or logical.

It's similar to a four-cylinder automobile engine: All four cylinders work and are equally important;

however, one cylinder fires first, before the others. Your primary clair drives the engine of your Divine guidance.

If you're naturally auditory, you already hear the voice of God and your angels. However, if this isn't your primary channel of Divine communication, you may struggle to pick up on Heaven's voice. You may read about accounts of people who receive warnings or messages from their angels, and wonder, *Why don't my angels talk to me?* Here are several methods that can help you hear the voice of the Divine, loud and clear:

— **Clear the ear chakras.** As we've discussed, each of the psychic senses is governed by a chakra energy center. Clairsentience (feeling) is regulated by the heart chakra, claircognizance (thinking) is connected to the crown chakra, and clairaudience (hearing) is governed by the two ear chakras. The next chapter will talk about the third-eye chakra's connection to clairvoyance (seeing).

The ear chakras are located above the eyebrows, inside the head. They appear to be a violet-red color. Imagine two violet-red disks spinning clockwise above your eyebrows. See or feel yourself sending them beams of cleansing white light and illuminating them from the inside. Notice how clean and large they're becoming. Repeat this method daily, or whenever you feel that your psychic hearing is clogged.

— **Release psychic debris.** If you've been verbally abused by others or by your own self-deprecating talk, your ear chakras are probably polluted with toxins from the negative words directed toward you. Mentally ask your angels to surround you with comforting energy. You can release the pent-up negativity in your ear chakras by writing down the names of those who've verbally abused you (including yourself) and putting the paper in a plastic container of water. Then, put it into the freezer compartment of your refrigerator. You'll have an immediate sense of release as you put these names in the freezer. Keep them there for a minimum of three months. (By the way, this is a wonderful method of releasing *any* kind of problem.)

— **Reopen tuned-out frequencies.** When you were a kid, did you tune out the voice of your mom, your dad, your teacher, or some other person— including yourself? As a child, your ability to shut out incessant nagging or other verbal unpleasantries may have been your only available defense mechanism.

The trouble is, though, you may have tuned out *all the other* voices in the frequency range of those you originally blocked. So you may have difficulty hearing a Heavenly voice that's in the same pitch or tone as your mother's, for instance. You might not hear your Higher Self's voice if you tuned your own voice out long ago. Fortunately, you can simply "change your mind" to reopen your physical and spiritual ears to the full range of frequencies. Since your firm intention to shut out sound was the origination of the blockage, simply make a different firm intention to now hear all ranges of sound frequencies.

— **Increase your sensitivity to sound.** Take time each day to notice the sounds around you. For instance, tune in to birds singing, children laughing, and cars driving by. Also, notice the sounds that accompany ordinary behaviors, such as turning the pages of a book, writing a note, or breathing. By paying attention to subtle and not-so-subtle sounds in your environment, you heighten your sensitivity to the voices of the angels and your guides.

— **Protect your physical ears.** As your sensitivity to the sound frequency of the angels increases, you'll find that loud noises bother you more than they did before. You'll need to cover your ears when you're in an airplane that's landing and avoid front-row seats at loud rock concerts, for instance. You'll also have to ask friends to speak more quietly to you on the telephone, request restaurant tables that are away from noisy groups of people, and secure hotel rooms positioned far from the elevator and ice machines.

— **Ask your angels.** Some people have quiet angels and introverted spirit guides. Just as you do when you're having a conversation with a living person, don't be afraid to ask whomever you're conversing with, "Would you please speak a little louder?" Our celestial friends really want to communicate with us, and they need our honest feedback to help guide them in knowing the best way to make their voices heard.

My mother, Joan Hannan, was having difficulty hearing her angels and guides, so she asked them to speak louder. But she still couldn't hear them, so Mom said in a powerful voice, "Please, speak even louder." She then heard her grandmother's voice say very distinctly, "I'm right here!" My great-grandmother seemed to mean, "You don't have to yell—I'm standing right next to you. I can hear you just fine!"

You're always in control of your Divine communication, and if you want Heaven to turn down the volume or intensity of your auditory messages, just ask. In the next chapter, we'll explore the world of clairvoyance and look at ways to help you see angels and Heaven-sent messages.

Chapter Eight

How to See Your Angels

The angels wish to connect with us visually as much as—or even more than—we wish to connect with them. They help us communicate with them by making their presence clearly known. My books *Angel Visions* and *Angel Visions II* (both published by Hay House) contain dozens of stories about people who've had sightings of angels.

What It's Like to See Angels

Many of my psychic-development students mistakenly believe that clairvoyance means seeing angels as distinct, opaque figures who look as solidly three-dimensional as living humans. They expect their visions to be outside of their head, instead of in their mind's eye.

Yet most examples of clairvoyance are similar to the mental pictures you see when you're daydreaming or having a nocturnal dream. Just because the image is in your mind's eye doesn't make the vision less real or valid. When I explain this to my students, they often exclaim, "Oh, so I *am* seeing angels after all!"

With clear intention and practice, most people can develop the ability to see angels outside their mental sphere with their eyes open. In other words, they're able to look at a person and see an angel clearly hovering over his or her shoulders. However, beginning clairvoyants usually must close their physical eyes while "scanning" someone. Then, in their mind's eye, they see images of that individual's guardian angels.

Some people see lights or colors in the initial stages of their clairvoyance. Others observe fleeting visions of an angel's head or wings. Some people see angels as translucent and colorless or opalescent, with shimmering hues radiating from them. Still others see them as full-figured beings, complete with brightly colored hair and clothing.

During stressful times or following intense prayer, some people will have a vivid angel encounter, similar to an apparition experience. While fully awake with their eyes wide open, the person sees an angel, who may look like a human being or take on a traditional angelic image, with a gown and wings. The angel is clearly there: The person may even touch or hear the being and not realize that it's a nonhuman until after it disappears.

Photography Orbs

One of the newest ways in which angels are showing themselves to us is by appearing in photographs as orbs of light. If you wish to see evidence of angelic beings, you can now see them in photographs! Their images appear as globes of white light when the pictures are developed. Fairies often appear in photos taken outdoors, and their images look like rainbow-colored orbs bouncing around fields and forests.

The best way to photograph these orbs is by taking a snapshot of a newborn baby or a spiritually minded person. Or try taking pictures when you're at a metaphysically related workshop, especially when the topic is angels. You'll find dozens of these orbs once the photos are developed. This method works best when you hold the intention of seeing the angels while you're taking the photos.

Just as with any other requests for your angels, mentally ask them to appear on film as you snap the pictures. The new digital cameras are especially successful at capturing angel images.

Other Angel Visions

Other ways in which we see the angels include:

— **Dreams.** Dr. Ian Stevenson of the University of Virginia has catalogued thousands of cases of "dream visitations" in which people have interacted with their deceased loved ones or angels while asleep. Dr. Stevenson says that the "degree of vividness" is the characteristic that distinguishes mere dreams from true visitations.[1] Visitations include rich colors, intense emotions, and a more-than-real feeling. When you wake from one, the experience stays with you longer than an ordinary dream. You may remember explicit details about it many years after it occurs.

— **Angel lights.** Seeing sparkles or flashes of light indicates that angels are nearby. You're witnessing the energy sparks as the angels move across your field of vision. This effect is similar to seeing sparks from the back of a car. It's simply friction, and it means that your spiritual sight is adjusted to viewing energy waves.

The colored lights emanate from archangels and ascended masters (my book *Angel Medicine* lists the various archangels and their associated aura colors). White lights are the glowing evidence of the presence of angels.

About half of my audience members around the world report seeing these sparkles and light flashes on a regular basis. Many people are reluctant to publicly admit this fact for fear that they're hallucinating. They're not. Seeing angel lights is a very real—and normal—experience.

— **Colored mists.** Seeing a green, purple, or other-colored mist is a sign that you're in the presence of angels and archangels.

— **Angel clouds.** Looking up in the sky and noticing a cloud in the shape of an angel is another way that the Divine beings let you know that they're with you.

— **Seeing signs.** Finding a feather, a coin, a stopped clock, or moved objects in your home; seeing lights flickering; or noticing other visual oddities lets you know that an angel is saying, "Hello, I'm here" to you. Deceased loved ones often make their presence known by sending birds, butterflies, moths, or specific flowers to you.

— **Having a vision.** Seeing a mental movie that provides you with true information about a person or situation, or that gives you guidance about your life purpose or making changes, is a sign of being in the presence of angels. So is glimpsing a brief image of something symbolic.

For example, when I meet a health-care worker, I invariably "see" a nurse's cap over that person's head. The angels often send this information to us—especially when we're striving to make the world a better place.

Seven Steps to Opening Your Third Eye

An energy center between our two physical eyes, known as the *third-eye chakra,* regulates the amount and intensity of our clairvoyance. Opening the third eye is an essential component of seeing across the veil into the spirit world.

Here are the seven steps to opening your third-eye chakra:

1. First affirm to yourself, "It is safe for me to see." Say this affirmation repeatedly, and if you sense any tension or fear while doing so, breathe deeply. With each exhalation, imagine blowing out your concerns about being clairvoyant (more information on releasing fears follows this section).

2. Take a clear quartz crystal and hold it in your dominant hand (the one that you favor when writing). Imagine a beam of white light coming from above and going into your crystal. Hold the intention that this white light is now clearing your crystal of any negativity it may have absorbed.

3. Raise the crystal, still in your dominant hand, until it's just slightly above the space in between your two eyebrows. Move your middle finger so that it's pointing through the crystal toward your third eye.

4. Then place the middle finger of your nondominant hand (the one you normally don't write with)

at the highest point on the *back* (not the top) of your head.

5. Imagine a powerful and bright lightning bolt coming from your dominant hand's middle finger, going through your third eye, and then ending up at your nondominant hand's middle finger. You're making a battery circuit, with your dominant hand sending energy and your nondominant one receiving it. As the power runs through your head, it's clearing away psychic debris and awakening your third eye. This process normally takes one to two minutes; and you may feel some pressure in your head, warmth in your fingers, and tingling in your hands. Those are normal sensations from the energy work involved.

6. Next, put your right hand above your right ear, still holding the crystal in your dominant hand. Do the same thing with your left hand and left ear. Imagine white light coming out of your dominant hand's middle finger. Slowly move both hands simultaneously toward the highest part of the back of your head. Keep repeating this motion seven times in a sweeping gesture. Hold the intention of hooking the back of your third eye (which looks just like the back of a physical eye) to the occipital lobe in your head.

This is the area of the brain that registers awareness and recognition of your visions. It looks like a thin, round skullcap that you're wearing angled on the back of your head.

With the white light, you're excavating a huge, five-inch chamber extending from the back of your third eye all the way to your occipital lobe. This chamber connects the flow of vision from your third eye to the visual part of your brain. In this way, you'll be more aware of the visions that you have, and you'll also understand their meaning.

I've worked with many people who had clean, open third eyes, yet they complained of having no, or limited, clairvoyance. *Having a clean, open third eye is not enough to ensure clairvoyance!* Without the connection between the third eye and the occipital lobe, a person wouldn't be aware of, or understand, his or her visions. It's like showing a movie without having the projector light on.

7. The final step is to put the middle finger of your dominant hand on top of the crystal, over your third eye (again, slightly above the area between your two physical eyes). You're going to lift any shields that you may have put over your third eye. With feathery, upward-stroking movements, coax the shield to

lift, as if you're opening a window blind. Be sure to breathe while you're performing this step, as holding your breath will slow the process. Repeat the shield lifting at least seven times, or until you sense that each shield is lifted.

You can perform this process on another person. If you know an individual who's spiritual and open-minded, especially someone who has experience performing energy healings, have them conduct this process on you. While these seven steps can be self-administered, their power is amplified when another person with clear intention (meaning, with a minimum of skepticism) performs them on you.

After you or another person go through these seven steps, you should notice a marked improvement in your mental visions. When you close your eyes and imagine a garden, you'll probably see stronger and more vivid colors and pictures than you did before the process. Your nighttime dreams may become more intense and memorable, and your photographic memory will most likely increase.

Again, the images you see may not appear as something outside of yourself. The mental movies may play on a screen that's inside your head. With practice, you'll be able to project and view those images outwardly. However, whether the visions are in your mind's eye or external is irrelevant. I find that my psychic accuracy is identical whether it's a mental image or something that I see outside of my head. The location of the vision isn't important. What matters is that you notice and give attention to the images, because they're so often visual messages from your angels.

Healing the Fear Blocks to Clairvoyance

If, after going through the seven-step procedure, you still find that your mental pictures are less than you desire in terms of size, clarity, or color, then you probably have some fears blocking you. These fears are entirely normal, and they can be easily cured whenever you're ready.

For instance, you may be afraid of:

1. Losing Control

The fear: You worry that if you open your clairvoyance, you'll be overwhelmed with visions of angels and dead people everywhere you go. You might also fear that God will try to control you or make unacceptable plans for you.

The truth: Clairvoyance is like a television set that you can turn on, switch off, and dim as you wish. And God's will for you is identical to that of your Higher Self. The Big Plan has lots of happiness and plenitude in store for you—plus, you'll find greater meaning in all areas of your life.

2. Seeing Something Spooky

The fear: You can't stand haunted houses or monster movies, and you don't want to see anything smacking of ghouls or goblins floating around your home.

The truth: If you've been able to watch the movie *The Sixth Sense* with your eyes open, you've seen the worst. The spirit world is beautiful, something that Hollywood hasn't caught on to yet. Even the Earthbound spirits and fear thought-forms (the so-called fallen angels) aren't half as bad as the average big-screen renditions of life after death. Most deceased people look radiant and youthful and exude happiness. Wouldn't *you* look wonderful if you knew you never again had to pay another bill?

3. Being Fooled

The fear: You have the worry "What if it's my imagination and I'm just making it all up?" or worse, "What if I'm contacted by lower-world spirits who are posing as my guardian angels?"

The truth: The reason why studies show that children have the most verifiable psychic experiences is because they don't get hung up on worrying whether or not it's their imagination. Joan of Arc is quoted as saying to her inquisitors, who asked her if she was imagining hearing the voice of God: "How else would God speak to me, if not through my imagination?" In other words, just because it's all in your head doesn't mean it isn't real, valid, or accurate.

Sometimes I'm asked, "Aren't you worried about being fooled by a demon masquerading as an angel?" This question implies that demons shop at costume stores, drape themselves in white feathers, and— boom!—wrap us around their claw-tipped fingers. The fact is that there *are* lower-world energies and beings whom I wouldn't invite to my home for dinner, just as there are living people whom I choose not to hang out with. But this is no reason to shield oneself from seeing clairvoyantly.

I mean, if I asked you if you'd rather walk down a dark alley on the wrong side of town at midnight or at high noon, naturally you'd say noon, right? And the reason? So that you can *see* who's there, of course! Well, the same holds true for the spirit world. Since those unsavory beings are there anyway, wouldn't you rather be able to glimpse who the players are so that you can call upon Archangel Michael to act as a "bouncer" at your home's front door, ensuring that no one gets through without proper ID—assuring that all visitors are beings of high integrity and a big inner light?

The inner light is the best indicator of a being's integrity, whether a living person or someone in the spirit world. With clairsentience, you can sense a person's character; with claircognizance, you just know that someone is of high integrity or not; and with clairvoyance, you can literally see the glowing light within.

So-called fallen beings in the spirit world can't mimic the huge glowing light that emanates from the belly and radiates upward and outward. These beings could put on an Archangel Michael costume, but they'd lack the essential element: the bright aura that results from living a life of Divine love. In this respect, clairvoyance helps us screen our friends in the physical *and* nonphysical worlds and actually keeps us safe from harm.

4. Being Punished for Something That May Be "Evil" or "Wrong"

The fear: You worry that clairvoyance is the devil's work and that God will punish you for sinning.

The truth: This fear is often based on Old Testament quotes warning about wizards, mediums, and speaking with the dead. Yet in the New Testament, we find Jesus and many others talking with the deceased—and to angels as well. Saint Paul, in his letters to the Corinthians, exclaimed that we all have the gift of prophecy and that we should aspire to these spiritual gifts . . . as long as they're used with love.

And that's the distinction, isn't it? The *Manual for Teachers,* volume III, of *A Course in Miracles* says that psychic abilities can be used in service of the ego (which it says is the only devil in this world) or of the Holy Spirit. In other words, we can harness clairvoyance for love or for fear. If you apply this tool in the service of God and for healing purposes, there's nothing to fear. You'll find that other people's judgments simply roll off of you.

5. Being Ridiculed

The fear: You're afraid of being dubbed "crazy," "weird," "a know-it-all," or "too sensitive" . . . or dealing with the judgmental attitudes of fundamentalist relatives.

The truth: You're probably a "lightworker" or an "Indigo Child"—that is, someone who feels compelled to make the world a better place from a spiritual perspective. Lightworkers—and their younger counterparts, the Indigo Children—very often feel that they're different or that they don't belong. When people tease you about your spiritual interests or gifts, it compounds that feeling even more. If you were teased during childhood, you may have unhealed emotional wounds associated with various types of ridicule. Ask your angels to intervene, and follow their guidance if they suggest that you seek professional help.

6. Taking Inventory of Your Current Life

The fear: You're afraid of being unprepared to make changes if you see something you don't like about your life—that is, you want to remain in denial.

The truth: Clairvoyance may increase your awareness of parts of your life that aren't working. It's true that taking an inventory may increase your dissatisfaction in certain ways; however, assessing your relationships, career, health, or some other life area doesn't require you to make an immediate 180-degree turn and fix everything at once. Dissatisfaction is a powerful motivator toward taking steps to improve things. It inspires you to take up jogging, eat more healthfully, see a marriage counselor, and/or devise other methods for healing your life.

7. Seeing the Future

The fear: You may be wary of foreseeing planetary or social changes that are frightening.

The truth: If you "see" these events, and you're absolutely certain that they aren't coming from your ego, then you'll have a better picture of your light-worker mission. You'll be specifically guided as to how you can help the planet avoid, or cope with, these changes. For instance, you may be called upon to pray for peace, send out healing energy, anchor the Light in various places, teach other lightworkers, or heal those who are affected by the changes.

While such an assignment may seem daunting and intimidating, remember that you signed up for it prior to your incarnation . . . and God and the angels wouldn't have given you such a monumental task unless they knew that you could do it. They also provide you with full support along the way—as long as you ask for it and are open to receiving that help.

8. Taking On Too Much Responsibility

The fear: Foreseeing a negative situation, you wonder, *Am I supposed to intervene?*

The truth: Earth angels are usually just asked to pray about a situation unless it's a very special assignment, and if you *are* supposed to intervene or warn someone, you'll be given very clear instructions about what to do.

9. Not Being Able to Do It

The fear: You worry that you're an imposter who's unqualified to be psychic or to perform spiritual healing. You wonder whether you really have any angels, and if you do, whether you'll be able to make contact with them.

The truth: Everyone feels like an imposter from time to time. Psychologists actually call this fear "the imposter syndrome." Research shows that some of the most competent, successful people are prone to experiencing this condition. It doesn't mean that you *are* an imposter; it just means that you're comparing your insides (which feel anxious in new situations) to everyone else's outsides (which appear to be calm, cool, and collected).

The ego, or lower self, uses sleight-of-hand fears such as this one to distract us from remembering who we are and from working on our life purpose.

Past-Life Blocks to Clairvoyance

Sometimes the block to clairvoyance is rooted in our distant past. Even people who don't believe in reincarnation will agree that significant events in history are still affecting our world today. One is the Inquisition, in which thousands of people were burned, hung, tortured, and robbed during the 15th century because they had spiritual beliefs or practices that were contrary to the reigning church. The pain of that event, and other "witch hunts" throughout history, still reverberates in the present day as ancient echoes that cry, "Conform to accepted beliefs or suffer the consequences!" Fear is the result, as well as "staying in the spiritual closet"—which leads you to keep your psychic abilities and spiritual beliefs a secret.

But how do you know if a past-life wound is blocking your clairvoyance? The signs include the following:

- You consider yourself to be nonvisually oriented—that is, you don't visualize easily, you rarely remember dreams, and you don't really focus on how people or things look.

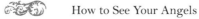

- You've had few, if any, psychic visions.

- You feel tense or worried every time you think about opening up your clairvoyance.

- You have an undefined sense of anxiety about becoming psychic, as though you'd get into trouble or be punished by some individual or even by God.

- When you think about people being burned at the stake or hung, your body reacts strongly with chills, shivers, breathing changes, or tension.

In contrast, here are the signs that childhood experiences have blocked your clairvoyance:

- You saw angels, sparkling lights, or deceased people when you were a child, but your psychic visions diminished as you grew older.

- You're a highly sensitive person.

- You were teased for being "crazy," "evil," or "weird" as a child or adolescent.

- You worry what your family would think if you revealed your psychic gifts.

- You're afraid that if you opened up psychically, you'd make life changes that would disappoint or harm your loved ones.

A past-life regression by a certified hypnotherapist, or via a vehicle such as my *Past-Life Regression with the Angels* CD, is the most effective way to release these blocks. Your unconscious mind won't frighten you with memories that you can't handle, so please don't worry that a regression will overwhelm you.

Trying Too Hard

By far the most common block to clairvoyance is trying too hard to see. As I touched on earlier, when we push or strain to do anything, we get blocked. That's because any type of pressure stems from fear, which originates in the ego—and the ego is 100 percent *not* psychic.

We try too hard when we fear, deep down, that we might not be able to achieve something and attempt to force it to happen. The underlying negativity, however, can undo hours of positive affirmations and manifestation efforts. The fear becomes a negative prayer that, unfortunately, attracts self-fulfilling prophecies.

Healing Psychic Blocks

Everyone has psychic blocks to one degree or another, so the point isn't to be completely clear of them . . . the objective is to be *aware* of them and deal with them promptly as they arise. Sometimes we become ashamed of our blocks, and we don't admit them to ourselves or others. Yet blocks are nothing to be ashamed of. They are, however, areas of our life that require our attention.

"Healed healers" (to borrow the term from *A Course in Miracles*) aren't people who are without issues—that would nearly be impossible in this world. Rather, they are those who are *aware* of their issues and strive to avoid letting them interfere with their Divine life mission.

Nonetheless, we can mend and release hang-ups that block us psychically. These healing techniques and tools can also have markedly positive results on other life areas, in addition to clairvoyance.

— **Healing during sleep:** When you're sleeping, your skeptical mind is also at rest. That's why it's a perfect time to engage in spiritual healing. With the skeptical mind asleep, your ego can't block the angels from performing miraculous clearings on you. So, as soon as you're ready to open up your clairvoyance, ask your angels and anyone else in the spirit world with whom you work to come into your dreams. An example of how to do so is to pray:

"Archangel Raphael, I ask that you enter into my dreams tonight. Please send healing energy to my third eye, and wash away any fears that could be blocking my clairvoyance. Please help me see clearly with my spiritual sight."

— **Cutting cords to family members:** If you realize that you're afraid of your mom's judgments about psychic abilities, for instance, you can use the cord-cutting techniques described in Chapter 5 and direct them specifically toward cutting the cords of fear connected with your mother. Repeat the process for any person (family member or otherwise) whom you worry about having a negative reaction to your clairvoyance. In addition, cut the cords with any individual from your past who ridiculed or punished you for being psychic.

— Support from like-minded souls: When I was preparing to "come out of the spiritual closet" and admit my clairvoyance publicly, I was naturally concerned about negative consequences. I was fortunate enough to become acquainted with a psychiatrist who was also acknowledging for the first time that he was a clairvoyant. Jordan Weiss was a university-trained internal-medicine doctor and a psychiatrist in private practice in Newport Beach, California. A recent head injury during an accident had opened up his third eye, and he found that he was able to see inside his patients' bodies. Dr. Weiss could also see the chakra systems and the negative emotions trapped inside of them. But he was afraid of openly admitting his clairvoyance, thereby risking his medical license and reputation.

We motivated, supported, and counseled each other with respect to going public about our clairvoyant gifts. We kept reminding one another that if we weren't true to ourselves, we really couldn't help our clients in the best possible way. Today, Dr. Weiss is completing his second book related to his psychic experiences as a psychiatrist.

I think *you* will also find it helpful to have the encouragement of someone else who's in a similar situation. Pray for such a person to come into your life, and you'll be guided to him or her. You can also consciously look for support at metaphysical meetings held at bookstores, New Thought churches such as Unity or Religious Science, psychic-development courses, or Internet bulletin boards related to the intuitive arts.

— **Sacred ceremony:** I've witnessed how these rituals help people release their psychic blocks. You can create your own sacred ceremony for the purpose of opening your clairvoyance. For example, write down a question for your angels such as: "What is blocking my clairvoyance?" Then record whatever impressions you receive. Afterward, light a fire in your fireplace or an outdoor fire ring. Meditate for a moment on letting go of the block written on the paper. When you truly feel ready to release it, throw the paper into the fire. You should feel a great sense of relief when you're done.

— **A past-life-regression session or CD:** About half of the psychic blocks that I see in my audience members stem from their past-life wounds related to

being psychic. As I mentioned earlier, it makes sense to go through a past-life regression to clear them. Most certified hypnotherapists are trained in giving such regressions. Your only task is to find one with whom you feel comfortable, because your trust in the regressionist is key to your ability to let go and allow your unconscious memories to surface. Alternatively, you can use a taped past-life regression such as my audio program produced by Hay House called *Past-Life Regression with the Angels.*

— **Positive affirmations:** I'm amazed by how many bright, knowledgeable metaphysicians complain to me that they're "just not visual." When I point out that this statement is a negative affirmation, they realize that these words are blocking their clairvoyance. Then they begin using positive statements to describe what they desire instead of what they fear.

"I am highly visual" and "I am profoundly clairvoyant" are examples of positive affirmations to say to yourself, even if you don't yet believe that they're true. Trust me—reality always catches up to your affirmed thoughts!

— **Calling on the angels of clairvoyance:** There are specialist angels for every situation, and psychic development is no exception. The "angels of clairvoyance" monitor and minister to your third-eye chakras, helping you develop spiritual sight. Mentally say:

> *"Angels of clairvoyance, I call upon you now. Please surround my third eye with your healing and clearing energy. I ask for your help in fully opening my window of clairvoyance now. Thank you."*

You'll probably feel tingles and air-pressure changes in your head—especially between your two physical eyes—as the angels of clairvoyance do their healing work.

— **Lifestyle improvements:** There's a huge correlation between how well you treat your body and the vividness of your clairvoyance. Your visions are always sharper, more detailed, and more accurate when you're engaged in a consistently healthful lifestyle. Exercise, proper rest, getting outside regularly, eating a light, plant-based diet, and avoiding toxins in food and beverages help you to be a clearer channel of Divine communication.

After using one or more of the preceding healing processes, your clairvoyance should be noticeably brighter and clearer. In the next chapter, we'll put it all together and look at how you can receive angel messages yourself or on behalf of another person.

Chapter Nine

Receiving Messages
from Your Angels

My life purpose isn't to give angel readings and spiritual healings to clients. It's to teach *other people* how to do these things for themselves and *their* clients. I always encourage my spiritual-counseling students to teach others—to create an ever-spreading ripple effect that increases the awareness that we *all* have angels, that we *all* can communicate with them, and that we *all* have spiritual gifts we can use to help ourselves and the world.

In this chapter, you'll read some of the exact steps I teach my psychic-development students so that you can give yourself and others angel readings.

How to Give an Angel Reading

An angel reading is similar to a psychic reading, except that you're directing the questions to guardian angels and spirit guides for the purpose of healing some life area and/or for guidance about someone's life mission.

It's best to give an angel reading to a person you don't know really well, someone who's open-minded and nonjudgmental. A new friend in a spiritual study group would be an ideal angel-reading partner. Still, you can definitely do a reading for a family member or old friend. It's just that your ego will scream at you: "You already knew that about this person!" If you can ignore the ego's rantings that "you're just making all of this up," you can give a reading to anyone, whether you know the person or not.

Let's begin with a mutual angel reading, where you and another person are reading each other simultaneously. Begin by saying a prayer to whomever you're aligned with spiritually, asking them:

*"Please help me to be a clear channel of
Divine communication. Please allow me
to clearly hear, see, know, and feel accurate
and detailed messages that will bring blessings*

to my partner and me. Please watch
over this reading and help me
relax and enjoy it.
Thank you, and amen."

Next, sit facing your partner. Then both of you should take a metal object from your body (such as a watch, ring, necklace, belt buckle, hair clip, glasses, or car keys) and hand it to the other person. Each of you should hold the metal object that you received from your partner in the hand that you normally don't write with. This is the hand where you receive energy—your "receptive hand."

Then, hold your partner's free hand with your own. Place your hands where they'll comfortably rest for the next few moments, such as on your or your partner's knees or lap. Now, I'd like to take you both on a vacation, okay? Please close your eyes and breathe in and out very deeply. . . .

Mentally imagine that the two of you are in an exquisite purple pyramid that has magically transported you to a white sandy beach in Hawaii. The purple pyramid lands with a gentle plop on the sand and opens up, forming a natural blanket for the two of you. It is a perfect day in

Hawaii, and since this is a completely isolated beach that's only accessible by boat or plane, you and your partner have total privacy.

You feel the gentle summer breeze blowing across your skin and through your hair. You smell the delicious salt air and hear the waves' melodic crash upon the shore. You feel a beam of sunlight dance warmly over the top of your head, as if it were going right in and illuminating the inside of your mind and body.

Off in the distance, you notice a pod of dolphins swimming playfully in the ocean. You tune in to these creatures, and you feel them send you a huge wave of Divine love energy. As your heart swells with warmth and gratitude for these beautiful animals and this perfect day on the beach, you realize that you're <u>one</u> with the dolphins. And then this realization extends even further: You are <u>one</u> with all of the life in the ocean—including the sea turtles and the colorful tropical fish—and you're also one with the waves, the sand, and the sun.

You realize that you're one with all of life, including your partner. And so you mentally affirm to your partner, <u>You and I are one . . . you and I are one . . . I am you . . . and you are me . . . you and I are one.</u> You realize that this oneness that you *share is real. Although you may look different on the outside, on the inside you and your partner truly do share one spirit, one light, one love. You mentally affirm to your partner: <u>One love . . . one love . . . one love.</u>*

As you revel in this knowingness, you also realize that you're one with all of the angels. As you scan your partner with your physical eyes closed and your spiritual sight wide open, imagine what it would be like if you could see your partner's angels in your mind's eye. What might they look like?

Do you see any that look like small cherubs? How about medium-sized angels? Really large ones? You might see these beings in full detail in your mind's eye, or as fleeting glimpses. Or, you might simply feel or know their presence.

As you continue to scan the space around your partner with your spiritual sight, you might also notice some people who appear to be deceased loved ones. The beings who stand directly behind your partner are usually the person's deceased parents. Do you see a man or a woman standing directly behind your partner? If so, notice any distinguishing characteristics, such as something unusual that he or she is wearing, eyeglasses, hairstyle, facial hair, eye color, or anything he or she is holding.

Then, scan around your partner's head and shoulders. Do you see people with light or gray hair who appear to have passed away when they were elderly? What other distinguishing features do you notice about them? How about any people who look as though they passed away when they were middle-aged? Anyone who passed away young? Be aware of details relating to anyone who appears to you, not worrying about whether you're imagining this or not.

Do you see any animals around your partner? Any dogs or cats? Any small or large animals? What do you notice about their fur? Is it light, dark, or multicolored? Long, medium, or short?

As you scan around your partner one more time, notice any other angels, deceased loved ones, or animals that may be present. If one or more of these beings especially attracts your attention, tune in to them now by holding the intention of connecting with them.

Even if you don't see anyone around your partner, or you're unsure of yourself, you can still receive accurate messages from your partner's guides and angels that will bring blessings to him or her. As you breathe in and out deeply, hold the intention of having a mental conversation with these beings.

Then, mentally ask them, <u>What would you like me to know about my partner?</u> Repeat the question as you take note of impressions that come to you in response. Be aware of any thoughts, words, mental pictures, or feelings that come to you as you continue to ask the question <u>What would you like me to know about my partner?</u> Don't try to force anything to happen. Simply trust that the answers are coming to you now, and notice even the subtlest little thought, feeling, vision, or word that you hear in your mind.

Next, mentally ask your partner's guides and angels, <u>What message would you like me to tell my partner, from you?</u> Again, be cognizant of any impressions that come to you as thoughts, feelings, visions, or words. Don't judge or discount these impressions. Simply view them with detachment.

Then, mentally ask your partner's guides and angels, <u>Is there anything that you'd like to tell me?</u> Be sure to breathe while you take heed of the answer.

Finally, mentally ask these guides and angels, <u>Is there anything else that you'd like me to tell my partner?</u> Again, listen for the response from many levels.

The most important part of giving an angel reading is having the courage to tell your partner everything that you received, even if you're unsure about the information or worry that it may offend the person (you can always pray for a diplomatic and loving way to deliver potentially offensive messages). While the angel messages may make no sense to you, they will probaby make perfect sense to your partner. Spend the next few moments, then, sharing everything that you saw, felt, heard, or thought during your mutual angel reading.

How to Do Automatic Writing in a Safe, Controlled Manner

The angelic messages in my book *Angel Therapy* were received through the process of "automatic writing." This is a method that allows you to transmit detailed messages from beyond. Sometimes people are afraid of automatic writing because they've heard stories about Earthbound spirits who come through these sessions pretending to be angels or master guides. However, there are ways to absolutely protect yourself against such occurrences, as you'll read later on.

You can conduct automatic-writing sessions with virtually anyone in the spirit world. It's a wonderful way to maintain and deepen relationships with deceased loved ones and to heal unfinished business and grief. If your heart is hurting because you've lost people dear to you, then you'll want to communicate with them through automatic writing.

You can use this technique to communicate with any of your deceased loved ones, even if they died before birth, as infants, or as toddlers. You can even contact those who spoke different languages, or who were retarded or mute. And you can even get in touch with your pets who've passed on. This is possible because our spirits communicate nonverbally and then "translate" these messages into our own native language. You'll probably notice, however, that your automatic-writing transmissions involve words that aren't a part of your normal vocabulary. You may find that your handwriting changes, and that you can suddenly spell words that you weren't able to before (and vice versa).

Automatic writing can also assist you on your spiritual path. For instance, through this method you can have conversations with God, your guardian angels, the ascended masters, and the archangels. You can ask your guardian angels, "What is your name?" and other queries. And you can request that the archangels and ascended masters help you remember, and work on, your life's purpose.

You can also use automatic writing to connect with a spiritual mentor. (See the full explanation of the Spiritual Mentorship Program in Chapter 6.)

You can handwrite your message or type it on a typewriter or word processor. If you're writing it by hand, you'll need at least four pieces of regular-sized paper, a firm writing surface, and a reliable writing utensil. It's a great idea to have some soothing music playing in the background and to adopt a comfortable seating position.

Begin your automatic-writing sessions with a prayer. The following is the one that I use before a session. It's based on my own spiritual faith, so you may want to rewrite it to fit *your* belief system. I would never tell anyone whom to pray to, but I do offer this prayer as an example of a way to effectively ask for help:

"Dear God, Holy Spirit, Jesus,
Archangel Michael, all of my guides, and all of
my angels, I ask that you watch over this automatic-
writing session and ensure that anyone who comes
through is a positive and loving being. Please boost
my ability to clearly hear, see, think, and feel your
Divine communication. Please help me accurately
receive these messages and bring forth those
that will carry blessings to me and to anyone
who may read them. Thank you, and amen."

Then, think about whomever you wish to connect with in Heaven. Mentally ask that being to have a conversation with you. You're going to pose a question and then write the response that you receive in a question-and-answer format, similar to an interview. The most important thing to keep in mind while doing automatic writing is to be completely authentic. Record whatever impressions you get, even if you're unsure whether it's your imagination or not. If you're getting nothing, write that down. You begin with jotting down whatever is occurring, and then eventually it switches over and becomes authentic spiritual communication.

During the automatic-writing session, you may feel as if someone else is controlling your pen or pencil. As I mentioned earlier, your handwriting, vocabulary, and spelling style will likely change during the session. Don't let this frighten you, as fear can block Divine communication. Remember, you're safe and protected by God and Archangel Michael (who is the "bouncer angel" and won't let any beings come near you unless they have loving intentions). Your hand may also start to doodle little circles, which is the spirit world's way of greeting you and saying, "We're so happy to connect with you!" If the doodling continues for too long, tell them that you're happy to connect, too, but would they please switch over to communication that you can understand.

Your ego may have a field day during your automatic-writing session. It might scream at you: "You're just making this whole thing up!" If that happens, put the burden of proof that you're receiving authentic communications on the being with whom you're conversing. Ask the being, "How do I know that I'm not just making you up?" The answer will likely convince you of the authenticity of your Divine conversation. If you're still not certain, though, keep asking until you receive a message that puts your ego to rest. Or, ask the being to give you a physical sign, and then stop writing. Once you receive that sign, you'll feel more confident during your next session.

Now, let's begin by having you think of a query that you'd genuinely like answered. Mentally ask the spiritual being this question. Then, write it down at the top of the page while mentally repeating it. Be optimistic, holding the positive thought that you'll be answered.

Record whatever impressions you pick up on through any of the four channels of Divine communication: thoughts, feelings, words, or visions. Then, ask another question and receive another answer . . . and so on.

When you're done writing to one being, you can switch to conversing with a different one. When your communications are complete, be sure to thank everyone involved. The angels say that they love to give us messages, and that doing so is inherently rewarding to them because it's fulfilling God's will. Yet, when we thank our angels, our hearts fill with gratitude. And that warm feeling of appreciation is the "I love you" that we exchange with our celestial guardians as a fitting finish to a love letter from Heaven.

Afterword

LETTING HEAVEN HELP YOU

Anyone can receive messages from their angels. In fact, we're all doing so . . . *right now.* If we aren't able to understand these messages, we can ask our angels for assistance, as well as use some of the methods outlined in this book.

When we ask our angels for guidance or for answers, we aren't bothering them. They want to help us with every area of our lives because they hope to bring peace to our planet one person at a time.

If you think that you'll feel more peaceful if you receive financial assistance, enter into a great love relationship, or secure a better job, then the angels are helping you with a sacred mission indeed. There's no request that's too trivial or too monumental for the angels. You aren't pulling them off of a more important task when you ask for their assistance. After all, the number of angels available to help far exceeds the number of people making such requests. There are billions of angels who are "unemployed" and bored who'd love to help you create a more meaningful and fruitful life.

Know that you deserve love, attention, and miraculous blessings from God and the angels. They love you unconditionally, no matter what mistakes you may have made in your life. You're just as special as anyone else who has ever lived. If it helps, remember that the Creator made us all equally wonderful. To put yourself down is actually to put down God.

The ego tries to convince us that we don't warrant help or attention from Heaven—that we're somehow bad or unworthy. That's the ego's attempt to prevent us from remembering our true spiritual identity and power. Please don't listen to that voice, because it could delay you from working on your life purpose. And we all need the fruits of your mission on this planet.

Allow yourself to be open to the messages from your angels. They won't tell you anything that you can't handle. They won't try to control your life, either. Their messages always help you feel safer and happier and make every aspect of your life more meaningful.

You can call additional angels to your side (or to that of your loved ones) simply by holding the thought that you'd like to be in contact with more of them. You can voice this request directly to God or to the angels. The result is the same, since the angels are extensions of the Supreme Being. They're literally God's thought-forms of love. Ask for as many as you'd like for yourself or another.

The angelic realm is filled with celestial beings specializing in every human condition. You can ask for angels to help you find a new home, locate a soul mate, or heal your body. There are angels who can aid you with parenting, with school, and with increased motivation to exercise. These Divine helpers want to assist you and give you messages, if only you'll let them. And the more you allow Heaven to help you, the more resources you'll have to give back to the world.

When you develop the habit of getting your angels involved in every area of your life, you'll function like a member of a successful sports team. You aren't giving the angels complete responsibility for your life—you're simply passing the ball back and forth between your teammates in Heaven. When you do this continually, life becomes so much simpler and more peaceful.

While suffering does foster spiritual growth, contentment creates even more. You learn through peace—and more important, you can better teach your children and others when you're in a state of joyful relaxation. You don't need to suffer for the sake of growth! God certainly doesn't want you to endure pain, any more than you want your own children to do so.

Remember, your angels love you, and they want to help you with anything that will bring you peace. Just ask them, and then follow the Divine guidance that they give to you in response to your questions. As you talk with and listen to your angels, you'll find everything in your life soaring Heavenward.

By tuning in to the messages from your angels, you *can* help create a peaceful world . . . one person at a time . . . beginning with *you!*

ᴇɴᴅɴᴏᴛᴇꜱ

Chapter Four

1. West, D. J. (1960). "Visionary and Hallucinatory Experiences: A Comparative Appraisal." *International Journal of Parapsychology,* Vol. 2, No. 1, pp. 89–100.

2. Stevenson, I. (1983). "Do We Need a New Word to Supplement 'Hallucination'?" *The American Journal of Psychiatry,* Vol. 140, No. 12, pp. 1609–11.

3. Osis, K. and Haraldsson, E. (1997). *At the Hour of Death.* Third Edition (Norwalk, CT: Hastings House).

Chapter Eight

1. Stevenson, I. (1992). "A Series of Possibly Paranormal Recurrent Dreams." *Journal of Scientific Exploration,* Vol. 6, No. 3, pp. 282–289.

About the Author

Doreen Virtue is a clairvoyant doctor of psychology who works with the angelic and elemental realms. She delivers their messages of guidance and inspiration through her writings and workshops. Her work includes the *Daily Guidance from Your Angels* book and oracle cards. Doreen is a frequent guest on international television and radio talk shows—with appearances on *Oprah,* CNN, *The View, Good Morning America, Richard and Judy, Kerry Anne,* and other programs. Her work has been featured in international newspapers and magazines.

A former psychotherapist who holds Ph.D., M.A., and B.A. degrees in counseling psychology, Doreen is a lifelong clairvoyant who came fully out of the "spiritual closet" and began openly teaching about angels following a brush with death in 1995. She gives workshops around the globe, including Angel Therapy Practitioner® Certification courses. For information about Doreen's workshop schedule, please visit her Website at: **www.AngelTherapy.com**.

You can listen to Doreen's live weekly radio show, and call her for a reading, by visiting **HayHouse Radio.com**®.

Notes

NOTES

NOTES

NOTES

NOTES

NOTES

We hope you enjoyed this Hay House book. If you'd like to receive our online catalog featuring additional information on Hay House books and products, or if you'd like to find out more about the Hay Foundation, please contact:

Hay House, Inc., P.O. Box 5100, Carlsbad, CA 92018-5100
(760) 431-7695 or (800) 654-5126
(760) 431-6948 (fax) or (800) 650-5115 (fax)
www.hayhouse.com® • **www.hayfoundation.org**

Published and distributed in Australia by:
Hay House Australia Pty. Ltd., 18/36 Ralph St., Alexandria NSW 2015
Phone: 612-9669-4299 *Fax:* 612-9669-4144 • www.hayhouse.com.au

Published and distributed in the United Kingdom by:
Hay House UK, Ltd., 292B Kensal Rd., London W10 5BE
Phone: 44-20-8962-1230 • *Fax:* 44-20-8962-1239 • www.hayhouse.co.uk

Published and distributed in the Republic of South Africa by:
Hay House SA (Pty), Ltd., P.O. Box 990, Witkoppen 2068
Phone/Fax: 27-11-467-8904 • www.hayhouse.co.za

Published in India by: Hay House Publishers India,
Muskaan Complex, Plot No. 3, B-2, Vasant Kunj, New Delhi 110 070
Phone: 91-11-4176-1620 • *Fax:* 91-11-4176-1630 • www.hayhouse.co.in

Distributed in Canada by:
Raincoast, 9050 Shaughnessy St., Vancouver, B.C. V6P 6E5
Phone: (604) 323-7100 • *Fax:* (604) 323-2600 • www.raincoast.com

Take Your Soul on a Vacation

Visit **www.HealYourLife.com®** to regroup, recharge,
and reconnect with your own magnificence.
Featuring blogs, mind-body-spirit news, and
life-changing wisdom from Louise Hay and friends.

Visit **www.HealYourLife.com** today!